CONFLUENCE

CONFLUENCE

navigating the personal & political
on rivers of the new west

zak podmore

TORREY HOUSE PRESS

SALT LAKE CITY • TORREY

First Torrey House Press Edition, October 2019
Copyright © 2019 by Zak Podmore

Published by Torrey House Press
Salt Lake City, Utah
www.torreyhouse.org

International Standard Book Number: 978-1-948814-08-9
E-book ISBN: 978-1-948814-09-6
Library of Congress Control Number: 2019932477

Cover art "White Canyon" by Julia Klema
Cover design by Kathleen Metcalf
Interior design by Rachel Davis
Distributed to the trade by Consortium Book Sales and Distribution

For Ruth,
the mother who raised me in desert canyons

CONTENTS

ELWHA RIVER

WHITE MESA URANIUM MILL
SAN JUAN RIVER BASIN

CATARACT CANYON
COLORADO RIVER

DOLORES RIVER

LITTLE COLORADO RIVER

COLORADO RIVER DELTA

RIO GRANDE RIVER

Wherever the river flows, it will bring life.

—Ezekiel 47:9

It's early summer and the water is high. My mother grasps the handles of two wooden oars and feels the Colorado River surge through her arms. A gray ring of raft surrounds her, sixteen feet from bow to stern, and beyond it, the mud-red river roils. Near the bow, her friend and former college roommate sits on a cooler. They're raft guides out for a week in Utah canyons with no clients, and they're nearing the crux of the trip: a feature known to river runners, in both fondness and fear, as Satan's Gut. Directly downstream the Gut heaves in a gnashing pit of foam large enough to swallow a Winnebago. River and air are locked in combat. The water billows up in angry clouds that never manage to sail into the sky but are pulled under again and again. Other boats in their party have already disappeared beyond the maelstrom.

As the current gathers speed, the world tilts. The first waves at the top of the rapid crash over the gray tubes and the raft fills like a bathtub. That morning the boat's load of army-surplus ammo cans—packed with apples, peanut butter, and beer—were lashed to the metal frame under a net of faded webbing. Now they float beneath their restraints. The woman in the front of the raft stands knee-deep on the floor and bails with a five-gallon bucket twice before sitting back down and grabbing onto a strap.

Bracing her feet against a box, my mother pulls back on the Douglas fir oars so they bend against the water. Deep in the woodgrains, fibers creak and snap. But the raft's course can't be *altered. The front tubes cross the upstream edge of the hole and the boat tips smoothly into its mashing heart. A white wall of water rolls across the bow and smacks my mother square in her lifejacket. The boat, more ballast than flotation, barely slows as the oars are ripped from her hands.*

The raft continues downstream. My mother does not.

She circles in the hole three times like a paper bag blowing through a culvert. As if compelled, she folds her knees to her chest and lets a deeper current pull her far below the roar. Ears pop as knees graze the limestone cobbles imbricated along the river bottom. All at once, it is quiet, dark, calm—even peaceful. She tumbles and does not know which way is up. Her lifejacket doesn't seem to, either.

She was twenty-five then, my sister and I still dreaming in the void of uncreation. When she'd tell the story to me later, she'd always gloss over her time underwater, but I could tell by her face that lifetimes were contained in the minute or two she spent beneath the Colorado River, that severed umbilical cord which once ran from the Rockies through the desert to the sea. I do not know what thoughts moved through her mind while she was submerged. I do not know what messages were pressed to her eardrums, what visions played through the pressure on her eyelids. But I'm aware that such moments are rarely silent; there is an abyss between the surface realm of the rower and the underworld of the swimmer. Over a life of river running, I've crossed that gap more than once. Time begins to stretch and bend below the surface. Unheard voices start to speak, even if their words cannot be repeated after breaking back through to the sanity of the day. As my mother sank all those years ago, I wonder what lights shone in the galaxies of her memories. Or was it all darkness—a wash of panic? It's too late to ask her now.

She did tell me the story's conclusion, though. Just as her searing lungs felt they could take no more, the river released its grip. The current slackened into a calm pool beyond the rapid, and the foam flotation around her chest began to propel her upward as if it were attached to the sky by a string. Her head broke through and dry air screamed into her lungs. Rescue ropes came slinging across the water from the half-circle of rafts around her.

There she was, located again, neck-deep in a river that carves through the bottom of the Colorado Plateau. The sun blazed on the broken stone blocks that spilled down from the canyon walls. The sediments in the river swirled like high country emissaries from the Never Summer Range, the Uintas, Abajos, La Sals, Wind Rivers, and San Juans. All around, dry washes tipped steeply toward the Colorado as if the arid landscape were bowing to the river, to the surging rapid, and to my mother, alive.

HOME SOMETIME TOMORROW

Spring 2017

The world moves past at two miles per hour. Outside the van window, clusters of gray-green sagebrush fidget on roadside dunes as wind whistles through the door gaskets. My pen scratches across a notebook page while Ute Mountain Ute councilwoman Prisllena Rabbit speaks to me about her homeland, the traditional hunting grounds of her relatives not far from the road.

"When the grandmothers—when Thelma—tells me I need to be somewhere, I listen," she says. Her hands are folded on her lap. An ink-drawn bear snarls from her T-shirt underneath the words "White Mesa Says NO to Uranium." Prisllena is serving her second term on the tribal council in another reservation town, but Thelma, who is two rows ahead of us in the fifteen-passenger van, lives nearby. She's a respected matriarch in the three-hundred-person village of White Mesa. Her short black hair and large turquoise earrings are visible above the seatback. Through the windshield, tufts of grass, already yellow in late spring, lay down in the gusts of wind.

The van creeps along at an idle, matching the pace of the ninety protesters spooled out before us on the highway shoulder. I don't need to ask any questions. Prisllena keeps on talking and she is not someone you interrupt. "The Creator made us a unique kind of being," she tells me. "Look at how long our lifespan is compared to other animals. That gift allows us to step onto the land and respect it—and then leave it alone. We need natural elements to survive—wood for cooking and medicine from plants. But we borrow with respect for our neighbors, the bear and other animals, and the water. How does a human—how does anything—survive without water?"

Two men at the front of the procession carry flags bearing the seal of the Ute Mountain Ute Tribe. They turn across the highway and onto a side road. The protesters follow, marching toward razor-wire-topped gates that guard a cluster of beige, metal-sided buildings. A dust devil pulls up a cone of red earth from a freshly bulldozed mound beyond the fence. Prisllena stares out the window at it as the van creeps to a stop. Someone slides the door open. A protest chant blows into the vehicle along with a plume of dust.

Two white pickup trucks are parked diagonally across the road a few hundred yards from the fenceline, and a man leans against each vehicle with folded arms. As the crowd approaches the roadblock, the men move into the path and stand their ground. The flag-bearers pause for a moment before they push past the pickups, the crowd pouring after them like floodwater between the trunks of cottonwood trees.

One of the men from the trucks yells to the other, "Call the cops!" But the cops are on their way. Flashing lights part the stream of people and they've soon headed off the flag-bearers. A white sheriff's deputy and a Bureau of Indian Affairs officer jump from their cruisers and this time the marchers stop, pressing against an invisible line set by the authorities.

"This is a private road," the handsome man in the blue BIA uniform shouts over the wind. "Turn back to the highway."

"We're going all the way to the gates. You can't stop us!" a protester says. I recognize him from earlier that morning: Thelma's son. Others shout in agreement. Someone reels toward the officers and is pulled back by a friend. The white deputy's hand moves slowly, as if through liquid, until it rests on top of his gun.

"If you go any further, you'll have to be decontaminated," the BIA officer says.

"Did you hear that? He said it's contaminated over there!"

"No, I said, if you go any further you'll have to be cleared. Legally. For radiation," the officer tries to clarify.

"We got it on film. He said 'contaminated.' He admitted it!"

Thelma steps up to the deputy, her face level with his Kevlar vest. She looks him in the eye and speaks in a voice rich with the inflections of the Ute language. "We've been inhaling the wind that kept going toward our reservation," she tells the deputy. "You people in Blanding, you don't even care about us. You don't give a shit about us. So here I am, I'm raising my voice."

The deputy is silent, frowning. The last name on his uniform identifies him as belonging to a deep-rooted Mormon family that arrived in the canyons of southeast Utah in the late 1800s. His ancestors built stone houses on Diné (Navajo) lands, plowed fields into Ute hunting grounds, and later worked in the mines alongside Ute and Diné people who were struggling to survive in the world the newcomers had brought with them.

Upwind, beyond the fence, is the last operational uranium mill in the country. Built forty years earlier, it was placed just outside the borders of the Ute Mountain Ute reservation.

Other tribal leaders offer speeches to the wind. They speak of deadly air and poison water. They speak of relatives. Of battles and fights. Of winning. And everyone speaks of home, of homeland, not as a place that was conquered or settled in some recent memory but as their ancestral birthplace, where the Ute Mountain Ute people have been since the beginning and the place where they intend to stay.

I float on the edge of the crowd and listen. Poisoned water worries me; the same aquifer that feeds the Ute town also flows from my faucet. But I can always run, and knowing this is what brought me to the protests. I've lived just south of the Ute reservation for three years. Though I also intend to stay, what would it feel like if leaving were impossible? I want to understand this word: *homeland*. I want to believe that this is home. Most of the people around me, it seems, have grown up out of the ground. They belong here. The bones of their grandparents rest nearby. But I was born without a history. I drifted into this place like the dust passing through the fence, and now that I've settled onto this patch of desert I want to avoid being swept away again.

Bones.

Certain clans of the Ute Mountain Ute people have a story that has found its way into the pages of books: In the beginning the Creator gave Coyote a pouch and told him to travel to a sacred valley. "Don't open it before you get there," Creator said. Of course, this instruction was unbearable. Coyote was only just out of sight when he unsealed the bag. People poured forth from the opening. They scattered into the hills, speaking strange tongues, and though Coyote gave chase, he was unable to catch them. Distraught, he clamped the bag shut and walked the rest of the way to the valley. There he emptied the pouch and this time, out came people speaking a language he understood: Ute. When Coyote returned to Creator and admitted what he had done, Creator told him that the ones who had escaped were now destined to be the enemies of the chosen Ute. These adversaries with their foreign languages—what did they speak? Navajo? Spanish? English?—would forever encroach on the homeland and threaten the blessed people.

Before there was a home, there were enemies.

(I moved to Utah a few years ago. Those who share my white skin and fair hair settled here 150 years before that. Is it possible we weren't the last to arrive, but, by way of some devastating accident, the first? Those who escaped Coyote's bag in the beginning?)

The elders lead the group away from the mill and back to the shoulder of the highway. Before we get there, angry words break loose near the pickups, which are still parked across the road. A younger Ute man with long dark hair spilling from a backwards baseball cap stands chest-to-chest with one of the white mill workers. "You're trying to kill us with your mill," he shouts. "You're trying to get rid of us, but it's not going to happen. We're not leaving."

The worker keeps his voice even, calm. "No need to get worked up, buddy." He offers a stiff smile. "We went to high school together. Remember? We were fine then. We're not out to get you."

Spectators form a half circle around the two men, leaving plenty of space between. A white woman with dreadlocks yells "Shame!" at the mill employees.

Another woman leans to my ear and gestures to the smiling worker who is still talking to the Ute man. "That's the mill manager," she says.

A line of protesters by the highway sings the quavering notes of a traditional song. Fists shoot into the air. Words that Coyote would have understood float above the crowd and are ripped away by the wind.

Another story: The enemies that escaped from Coyote's pouch amassed and threatened the Ute people like never before. The Ute warriors fought to the very brink of defeat and all seemed lost. But just in time a giant appeared. He towered over mesa tops and waded through the clouds. He joined the fighters and drove the evil back. Victorious, the people celebrated and thanked the warrior. It was only then that they realized he had been gravely wounded. He lay down on the land to rest, his arms folded over his chest, and turned to stone. Juniper and fir grew on his body. Deer and bear came to live there. Snow fell on him in the winter and the people moved their wickiups around his great shoulders. The warrior is still visible in the homeland—the Ute Mountain for which the people are named. There he sleeps, waiting for the next battle.

The protesters have left. I stand talking to the mill manager as the clouds glow pink above Sleeping Ute Mountain. He tells me a different kind of tale. He speaks of hard work, of pioneers, of men who prayed and pushed their bodies and their tools against the earth, day after day, year after year, generation after generation, and made it work here in this harsh land. The mill offers work, he says. It allows people to continue making a life here. His strong freckled arms are still crossed on his chest. He uses the same word as the Ute councilwoman. *Home.* He says the mill allows people to stay here and raise families, to stay here at home instead of moving off to some city to find a job.

His boots are dirty and his shirt white. He asks how long I have lived in Utah and I tell him.

"Three years, huh?" he says, sounding exhausted. "Well, I guess everyone wants to move here now." He tells me his great-great-grandfather settled the tiny town where I live. His relatives no longer reside there, but many newcomers do. I can see he doesn't want me in Utah, but he's not cruel about it.

I could tell him that I've been coming here my whole life or that my parents moved to a town on the other side of Sleeping Ute Mountain thirty-five years ago. I could tell him that when my girlfriend, Amanda, got a job here, we both decided our first week that there was no place we'd rather live. I could explain how we were married last year in a redrock canyon outside of town, and that we've moved into a small home near the San Juan River. I could say we never want to leave.

Instead, I tell myself that he is right. I am a typical white American, someone who moves in but does not stay. I know that this land was promised to his people, not to mine. His Mormon ancestors tried to escape America and create their own kingdom in the desert. They partly succeeded. The town where he lives serves no alcohol; even the grocery store closes on Sunday. In the story he tells, the mountains do not come to life, but in their way they still provide for his people. We shake hands but keep talking.

As he recounts the hardships of his pioneer ancestors, we lean against his truck and stare out over the sagebrush dunes to the blue domes of a mountain range and the outlines of mesas on the horizon. The hills roll gently away from where we stand, hiding the incisions of a hundred canyons that bore into mountain flanks and sever veins of uranium that run through the rock below our feet.

It is 1879 and church leaders direct a band of devotees to settle in southeast Utah, in part to bring a peaceful solution to the raids Ute, Paiute, and Diné warriors are making on Mormon settlements. Brigham Young, the recently deceased prophet, had said it is "cheaper to feed than to fight them," and the new leaders agree. The Book of Mormon, translated from golden tablets found buried in the hills of upstate New York, has been on paper for forty-nine years. Indians, according to the tablets, are members of a wayward Israeli tribe who strayed from the righteous path long ago and who were cursed with dark skin. It is written, however, that they will one day return to church teachings and become "white and delightsome" people. It is a matter of duty for the devotees to convert, to save, to civilize. The faithful spread through Utah's redrock country to feed and redeem its lost inhabitants.

A brave group of Latter-Day Saints agrees to heed the leaders' command to cross southern Utah, and more than 230 people gather to form a wagon train. They take livestock and seeds and expect the journey to last six weeks. Their crossing is not easy. Canyons block the way. Mesas stretch flat then fall away all at once. The pioneers spend weeks blasting a path through a notch in the cliffs above the Colorado River, at times constructing platforms of timber to hold up the wheels of the wagons as they rattle over an otherwise sheer drop-off. Starving livestock feed the expedition, and no Saints die. On the trail, two children are born.

Six grueling months after setting out, what becomes known as the Hole-in-the-Rock Expedition stops twenty miles short of its destination and its members found the village of Bluff where the San Juan River has carved a wide valley between walls of sandstone. The Diné herders and the few white Gentile families who already live near Bluff do not understand why the newcomers with their cumbersome wagons didn't follow older, easier routes to the north or south. But, for the Saints, it was all part of the plan. The Heavenly Father had tested them, but because of their faith He had delivered them safely. They had struggled and triumphed. And didn't this mean that the faithful were now entitled to the land?

They multiplied. As the years passed, the settlers' bones went into the ground. Near my house, a rectangular stone pillar marks where one of them is buried. On the front: a man's name. On the other three sides: the names of his three wives and their many children.

Year after year the silty river overflowed and filled in the irrigation ditches of the Saints. Floods rampaged down canyons and knocked over the homes they'd made of quarried sandstone. A fire consumed the town hall. The Navajo Nation was expanded following the arrival of the Saints so that the river became the boundary between peoples. Colorado cattle companies pressed into the Utah Territory. Hungry, exhausted, and surrounded, the children of the pioneers eventually abandoned Bluff for higher ground, carrying with them the story of their miraculous arrival.

Now restaurant owners inhabit the sturdy stone houses built by the pioneers. Artists and archaeologists grow green chilies in backyard plots. The irrigation ditches remain dry.

The trucks come in along the tangled roots of highway that hold this country together. They roll across many states, across the northern border, bearing loads that glow through Geiger-counter screens. Laws regulate where you can put this waste, and the laws cause problems for those who want to get rid of it. But there is a solution. If you call it "alternative feed" and run it through a mill to extract the elements of the bombs we say we'll never use, the laws see the loads differently. And then the waste can pass through evaporation ponds and into storage mounds topped with crushed gravel where it is said the waste will stay put for centuries.

There is only one uranium mill left in the United States, and it is on the border of Ute lands. It's a mill calibrated to perform a legal alchemy that allows the useless waste to come to rest underground. But beneath the surface, those burials twist like troubled spirits. They rise and return to the wind. They search underground for water and every year the samples turn up more proof of this movement—heavy metals, chloroform, radioactivity. Below the mounds lie older burials still, bones that moan in the dark earth.

Dust.

(My first memories are of dust swirling in the light. I am dropped in the world near a river, a juniper tree, the red dirt of an old uranium-mining road. My mother has my hand. She's leading me around a rapid which roars up through the trees. I steal a glimpse of it—whitewater, foam, chaos. But through the branches the light is silent, cottonwood tufts and dust particles ride toward the cool air of the river across spangles flung on the ground. My mother is all of this. The warm hand knowing where to go. The serenity of the light. The path around the danger.)

A month after the march, one hundred people file into a brown building in Blanding and sit on metal folding chairs. Many people from the protest are there. As the Ute man who went to high school with the mill manager speaks, he notices that no one will look at him. They lower their heads. He speaks about his uncle who fought years ago to stop mill tailings from being buried near the Ute lands. Who fought and won. Later, he tells me the people lowered their heads because they knew he was right: the mill has to go.

Other Ute locals address the room. They tell of children and elders on the reservation with asthma, leukemia, and lung cancer. They stammer and curse and yell. They speak about the dust.

(Another memory from that same year: light from the rising sun is falling through the window of the Colorado cabin where I grew up. I'm standing half-asleep on the stairs, stopped by motes disappearing through the line between shadow and day. I hear my mother weeping below me on the couch, my father too. They're in each other's arms. There has been a death. Steve. He breathed the dust in the uranium bust town of Moab, sixty-five miles north of Blanding. Asthma closed up his lungs. He suffocated in the sunlight. Thirty years old. I know the name but I don't understand what has happened. I climb onto my mother's lap and my tears darken into her shirt.)

Next a series of people from nonprofits in cities a few hours away take the microphone. They speak of fines and water-quality violations. They explain the geology below the mill, how a shallow aquifer with elevated levels of heavy metals rests above a deeper aquifer that supplies Ute communities with drinking water. They describe what's behind the fences of the mill: ponds with plastic liners, some of which had been rated to a twenty-year lifespan when they were installed thirty-five years earlier. They tell of a lawsuit which argues the mill is in violation of the Clean Air Act for excessive radon emissions. The lawsuit identifies an eighty-mile radius around the mill as a cause for concern. They say the Environmental Protection Agency lists radon as the second-leading cause of lung cancer in the United States after smoking.

(There was always dust in that house in Colorado. An unpaved road wrapped around it, and rolling tires kept the earth unsettled. The walls of the living room were set into the hillside a century earlier when the house was a stable for passing stagecoaches. And in the ground: uranium, an element which endures through branching of species, extinctions, ice ages, and rising seas. But even as it takes billions of years to decay, radioactive radon gas escapes from it each day; radon clings to dust particles, drifts through the air, settles on tabletops, flows into and out of lungs. Those particles rode in bodies, my family's bodies, as we ranged out into the world, seeds of mutations carried through life—to cross-country ski trails every winter and Utah canyons every summer. Earth becomes flesh, and flesh surrounds our bones. And eventually, bone burns back to dust.)

The mill has its defenders, too. It's a way of life, they say. The mill manager from the protest is at the meeting. He says to look at the facts. He wants to sound calm and reasonable. He says there are high standards for safety in place, plans for mishaps. The chemical spills still being pumped out of the ground are from decades ago. Technology has improved since then, he says, there is nothing to worry about.

Phil Lyman, the county commissioner, takes the stand. He alludes to the million-plus dollars Energy Fuels pays annually in taxes to local coffers. He talks about the jobs the mill provides: fifty to one hundred at any given time. The livelihoods. The way of life.

Lyman was arrested a few years earlier for riding an ATV down a road that had been closed to protect ancient burials, skeletons with ceramic pots resting on their chests. Roads are part of the way of life here, worth sacrificing your freedom to defend. The county spends six million dollars annually, about a third of its total budget, on road construction and maintenance. Thousands of miles of dirt tracks are kept graded and cleared each year. And from roads like these all across the Southwest rise plumes of red dust—billions of tons' worth according to United States Geological Survey studies—which float away with the wind and stick to Rocky Mountain snowfields. Spring runoff comes to Utah a month earlier than it used to; the dust-laden snow absorbs more sunlight. And the droughts come more often.

Bruce Adams, another commissioner, agrees with Lyman. He repeats these lines about jobs and taxes. He says he toured the facility a few years ago and was very impressed.

I recall a newspaper account, also from a few years ago, of a trip Adams took to a senator's office in Salt Lake City. He was there to beg for more funding for cancer screenings in his hometown. Adams grew up in Monticello, the county seat, in the 1950s and '60s. Those were boom years, and many still sing praises to the money that once poured in. It was the Cold War and Monticello was on the front lines. The town mill took ore and processed it into yellowcake and shipped it off to help stockpile the US arsenal. Some longtime residents, including Adams, told the newspaper reporter of hot summer days quenched with dips into the ponds beneath the mill. He remembers kids rolling down the sand of the tailings piles and others recall loading up trucks to make backyard sandboxes. Adams' friend died of leukemia before he graduated high school. Fifty years later a citizens' group recorded seven hundred cases of cancer among former residents of Monticello, a town which today has a population of two thousand. There were birth defects, more leukemia deaths, rare skin diseases. But skepticism is easy. Who can say which case of cancer was caused by uranium milling, which from background radon emissions, which from cigarettes, which from bad luck?

Adams doesn't mention any of this at the meeting. The White Mesa Mill cannot be compared to the mills of the Cold War. Those were different times. He toured the facility and was impressed.

Another series of newspaper articles tells this story: At one moment, headlights taper off into scrub oak. The truck cab hums with the sound of rolling tires—hours of boredom. Then, a deer. The driver finds the brake pedal and hits it hard. A mixture of baking soda, water, and uranium leached from Wyoming sandstone sloshes in the back of the truck. The deer scampers off and is gone. Three hundred miles later, the driver stops at the gates of the White Mesa Mill, and workers notice white stains of leaking radioactive fluid along the back of the truck. The load is lighter than it was in Wyoming.

Later, on a different truck, similar stains are seen at the same gates of the mill. A "faulty door in the truck container" is to blame. Whether the spills pose a hazard to towns or not is never fully settled. The Nuclear Regulatory Commission threatens a fine but company officials request to be spared of such overreaction. No fines are levied. The company promises to do better.

⌣

A white woman approaches the microphone. She's known as a local activist. She takes on the environmental groups and fights for local values. She says the mill helps hold the community together, and she doesn't see what the fuss is all about. She tells the audience she beat cancer. You can learn a lot from cancer, she says. We shouldn't be afraid of cancer, she says. Cancer can be a good thing.

Once again, the heads of the audience are bowed low.

Rivers.

The snows fell deep last winter and now the rivers are high. A great blue heron, driven off of the sandbars by the runoff, is starving near a camp of rafters. The high water has made fishing impossible, and the heron doesn't take to the air as the rafters spend an afternoon following an hour hand of shade around the base of a cottonwood. It crouches on the edge of the clearing, snapping up whole lizards with quick strikes of its neck. In its droppings: needles of bone.

My parents met in the early 1980s where the Great Plains buckle up against the eastern side of the Rocky Mountains. Their suburban teenage years—my father's saturated in tepid rebellion aided by Clash records and my mother's in Catholic school with a household full of eleven siblings—vaporized as they discovered backpacking trips through alpine meadows of columbines and, later, multi-day floats down the Colorado and Dolores Rivers. They ran the San Juan, launching in Bluff and floating along the north side of the Navajo Nation toward Lake Powell. This was unlike any life they had imagined, growing up. The hometowns they left behind were described to me as Sodoms and Gomorrahs, full not of sin and brimstone but of strip malls and car dealerships. To my young ears, they had the names of far-off lands: Long Island, the Midwest. I knew those were places we'd never return to live. Our home was where Colorado drops into Utah, here amid the redrock, muddy water, and night skies pierced with stars.

There were boom days. The war may have been cold, but the federal government paid handsomely for hot rocks. When it all ended, it wasn't clear who was to blame. Some blamed the feds and their arsenal for the teenagers lost to leukemia. Some blamed the feds for coming up with too many rules and killing the industry. Cal Black ran the San Juan County Commission as the boom days were fading. He prospected for uranium. Part of Black's revolution was to prove the obvious. A rock was a rock, and rocks weren't sinister. They were money, but they weren't dangerous. It's said he wore a bolo tie made with a chunk of uranium around his neck. He was a Westerner, part of the chosen clan. Black wasn't a fearful man. When cancer came for him, it was unrelated to the bolo or his years in the uranium mines. It was just his time to go.

Prisllena Rabbit listens to the elders. Her hair is black and glistening, her smile warm and gentle as she rides next to me in the van. She speaks about the enemies of the Ute people that Coyote released in the beginning. "The US government tried to eliminate us," she says without self-pity or malice. "They're still trying to eliminate us today with this mill. But we're not leaving. We're here to stay and to remain a process of life. We're here to speak for life around the uranium mill with human common sense. If you cut yourself, you're always going to have a scar."

My parents were married in the foothills of the Rockies and skipped their own graduation ceremony to keep moving west. On the Utah side of Colorado, where peaks slide into canyons, they parked my father's Dodge Dart on the banks of the West Fork of the Dolores River and pitched a tent.

Over the next few months, they built a yurt with the help of a how-to book and a truckload of canvas. The mountain stream which flowed past their front door plunged, within a few dozen miles, past the edge of the Colorado Plateau: wind-softened redrock and the boreholes of old uranium mines. Just up the river lived Steve, a friend from school who had grown up poor in Virginia, eating Wonder Bread and corn grits with his single mother. Two years into college, his estranged father died and left him with an incomprehensibly large fortune. So Steve bought a fleet of rubber rafts and a few outfitter permits from the Bureau of Land Management. He hired my parents to manage the company and his friends to work as guides. Often they had more guides on the rafts than customers, making week-long trips down the Dolores and San Juan and weekend floats down Westwater Canyon on the Colorado. Even with paying customers, Steve would always make the rounds the last day on the river, asking everyone on the trip if they had anywhere they really needed to be the following day. "We've got enough food," he'd say. "We can do a layover here and stay two more nights."

Between trips, Steve lived in a one-room cabin he built on the riverbank. A plywood outhouse stood back in a thicket between the cabin and my parents' yurt. One night the roof started leaking above Steve's bed, and he rigged up a tarp to funnel the flow into a bucket. The tarp worked so he never bothered to fix the roof.

My parents and Steve were the settlers who arrived after the wolves and grizzlies were all gone, here to harvest not beef, crops, or coal from the land but a new commodity: adventure.

When my mom and a friend wanted to learn to kayak in the frigid waters of the upper Dolores, they spent a few evenings sewing splash jackets by the light of kerosene lamp on a pedal-driven Singer machine that had belonged to my grandmother.

Each time my parents and Steve drove the company's retired school bus to the boat ramp, they'd pass dump trucks hauling fill. Cranes rose like crooked oil derricks from the riverside. The West's great rivers had all been dammed and the Dolores was last in line. Rainfall was never reliable on the edge of the desert, but the river swelled with snowmelt every spring. That water would be captured, stored, and piped out to bean fields. The plateaus would bloom like Eden.

The mill manager is proud of his garden, especially the slices of tomato so flavorful they make the cheeks ache. He feeds them to his girls, one and three years old. There are ears of corn in late summer, and spring radishes cut into salads of greens that his blond wife picks before dawn for the best flavor. "The wind blows right toward that garden," he says. "It blows from the mill right toward the garden and toward my house, not the Ute reservation. If it's not safe, I'll be the first to find out." He's not actually concerned that he will find out. He isn't afraid of working in the dust, and he isn't afraid of work. The money comes in, pays for his house and his garden. No water leaks from his roof. His heroes are the men who broke this land, dragged chains between bulldozers to level juniper forests, and pushed the cattle from red valleys, which offered far more rock than forage, up to mountain meadows at the right time of year. They planted big gardens and made it work, even in this desert, through work. He's proud of that. He's proud of his garden.

Before I was born, they came and killed the Dolores River. They plugged it up and turned it into a reservoir. The river once flowed through canyons just to the northeast of the sleeping warrior mountain, but now it is practically dry most years, a hot clear creek that has ceased to carve into the landscape. The raft companies, including Steve's, dried up and blew away.

As a child I was like a river: I refused to move in straight lines. My hero was a man who slept under a tarp and always wanted to live out of rafts for one more night. He was someone who never wanted money to ruin his work, and he never wanted his life to be lost to work. His early attempts at gardens failed. Deer nibbled off the first spring sprouts, or the summer squash wilted in the heat. He'd forgotten to water them. He was away too much, pushing rafts through whitewater and around boulders. There was nothing more to ask for, even as the dust blew in from Utah and his asthma attacks got worse.

From the edge of the mesa, it looks like a silver whale breaching in a shimmering sea of redrock: thousands of tons of crushed gravel dumped on the old uranium mill near Mexican Hat to keep the dust down. Before the gravel, in the fifties, the mines were busy and trucks would haul ore down rattling dirt roads from the high country to the mill. But just before they got there, they'd have to cross the San Juan River. The bridge was one lane and wooden. There was no guarantee it would hold a fully loaded truck. So the drivers would dump half of the ore on one side of the river, right there on the ground, and they'd take the other half to the mill before going back for the rest.

An old-timer in town laughs when he tells the story. "Yessir, a Geiger counter will probably still go crazy under that bridge."

In 1995, a few years after Steve choked on Utah's air and died, I peered down from the stairs again as a seven-year-old. My mother was on the same couch, my father by her side. They were schoolteachers now, not river guides. Our doctor friend and his sister, a midwife, sat by my mom's legs. They'd been there for hours and I'd gone up to bed and come back several times when sounds came through the walls. I'd spent months laying an ear to the white taut belly that was now seizing with strands of muscle. My mother's face was flushed, her head facing south. My father was crouched on the ground, and I saw his eyes close for a long minute. I wondered if he was praying, but I didn't know to what. I knew there was pain. I wasn't worried, though, because when my mother emerged from it for long enough to see me watching, she snatched a smile through the exhaustion. Through the window, the outlines of hills began to appear. In that early light there were first breaths, a short cry with dark pupils looking out for the first time. My father beckoned to me. I looked at the purplish skin, the eyes fighting to open under heavy eyelids, the expanding ribs.

"It's a Mollie," I said.

Over five hundred abandoned uranium mines are scattered across the Navajo Nation. For decades, chunks of uranium were laid into the foundations of hogans. The public health clinics still treat rare cancers each day and maybe it's related. In 2006 uranium mining was banned on the reservation. But prospectors still dig on sections of private land within the nation's boundaries. Trucks come down the highways trailing dust or sometimes a white line of leaking radioactive waste. Protectors with bandanas over their faces are traversing the route. They've known battle. Against coal. Against uranium. Against pipelines that now carry oil beneath rivers. They're training others. And when the shipments come across their land, they're preparing to lock themselves up: hands in PVC pipes, necks in chains wrapped to the metal of semitrucks. Up in San Juan County, Phil Lyman, descendent of the Hole-in-the-Rock pioneers and now county commissioner, reportedly says to a group of Diné activists, "You lost the war."

Not everyone is convinced the war is over.

Dust, river, window. Life passes in orbits. The vultures that circle my Utah home in the summer heat spin off to brood over Baja canyons before the nights begin to freeze. On the sea islands where they roost, the stones are plastered smooth and white.

My mother lay on the couch one final time on the last day of February in 2014. Her head was pointing north. Her belly was taut and white again. I'd laid my hands on it in the weeks before, resorting to spontaneous rituals of hope, asking that the mass growing on her liver would begin to shrink. Scans also revealed a small spot on the inside of a rib, a formless fly that refused to be brushed away. It started in her lungs and when it was discovered four months earlier it was already Stage Four.

On the hospital forms, she liked to answer the question that asked how many cigarettes she had smoked in her lifetime. She always checked the first box: zero to ten.

My father had our home tested. Radon, at levels beyond what they would allow if you were standing outside a nuclear power plant or a uranium mill, was radiating out of the stone walls cut into the hillside along the back of our home.

The dying took hours, days. We were by the couch all through that last night; we climbed and descended the stairs in shifts. She couldn't speak or move. The last afternoon, I was by her side, my hand on her body, my arm around my sister, nineteen years after she first saw the world in this very same spot. At the moment when our mother's chest ceased to move and her face tightened cold, I melted through the big glass window that let in the light to illuminate the dust. I floated then flew, looking down on the scene like a pinyon jay at the first green sprouts of the year glowing along the drifts of melting snow, the black leaves of last fall pasted to the ground, and above that, the red hillsides dotted with juniper trees.

Dust, bones, rivers.

We push into each other's territories. In a single landscape, tides of people ever rising. The light-skinned families from the east spread over this Ute and Diné and Pueblo land, disrupted hunting routes, and trampled over the ancestors' ground. They dried up my family's river and that water went to the bean farms of European-American settlers but also to the toe of the Sleeping Ute Mountain where it greened a patch of reservation and brought in jobs. Now the Ute community members speak out against the dust and the tailings creeping into aquifers. The white workers see a brewing battle for their homeland. They fear a future where real, honest work is an abstraction, where everyone is a hotel manager or a guide for tourists. A future where the farms are left uncultivated.

The mill manager is speaking. The protesters have all left. He is worked up; he says he was threatened by the Natives, but he must put on a brave face. He's not a fearful man. He says he would visit Chernobyl. He calls it a wildlife park. He says the radiation at Fukushima has killed no one. He says to look at the facts. Radon comes out of the ground. Uranium is in the earth. His grandfather, a uranium miner, died of lung cancer. But so have others who never got near the stuff, who never touched a cigarette. The sun gives you cancer, for Pete's sake.

We have our founding narratives. The reason why we're here and why we belong: the pouch Coyote opened too soon, the trail through the notch in the cliffs, the yurt beside a river. And many of us believe we know how the end will come—the chaos of a world on fire.

The Ute people say they've long known how to give as they take. Those who came later only took, even as they gave back to their own clan. And my people tried to only look, to see but not to touch. But all the time we were taking from somewhere else. We wanted adventure, not work. We wanted to leave only footprints. The land is here to sustain our spirits, we thought, but we were the first to assume that it didn't also have to nourish our bodies. Our gardens were small and we had to feed off the tendrils reaching through to the other side of the supermarket shelves. We pushed into the backcountry, the land that the Ute and Diné and Mormon people called home. We called it wilderness.

In the ground, the burials grow restless.

There's a windowless prison at the base of Sleeping Ute Mountain just north of the fields watered by the dammed river. You can come and go as you please, but you'll keep coming back. There are happy tunes and the sounds of clinking coins and the gaping jaws of people who have sat too long without blinking. There are no guards, just the songs and the screens flashing joyful colors. The buttons read MAX BET and SPIN. The chairs are sticky. There's no booze here, only complimentary soda and coffee, but the place is still packed.

In the parking lot, I see a prudent man step out of an ancient Econoline van, the paint chipped off to reveal continents of bare metal. A single green bale of alfalfa is tied to the roof rack—for the sheep back home. Best to buy the necessities before entering the place where you emerge with only the memory of a paycheck. I met the man that sold him that alfalfa a few months earlier, a Diné grandfather with a wide smile all gums and a few blackened stubs of teeth. He said his relatives were fools. They worked all week and drove to the windowless building to donate all the money they earned to the Ute people, who were never too fond of those from the Navajo Nation and vice versa. ("If Sleeping Ute had been Diné," an old Navajo joke goes, "he would have gotten up and gone to work.") I dip into the maze of machines behind the driver of the Econoline and in that bustling building I see only a handful of *bilagáanas*, white ones.

We traveled down the Colorado River for two nights with a box carrying the dust of my mother and the flecks of her bones. My father was sick outside of his tent the night before we released her. He insisted his sickness was caused by a real parasite, a physical problem. Not by this other problem of a wife in a box lined with a plastic bag beside a river.

She had asked to be released in the Colorado. *When I die let my ashes float down the red river, let my soul roll on down to the Utah state line.* We'd been here together a hundred times as a family, the borderlines of our life, the place where the river runs west, where mountain water flows into streaked terracotta canyons and in them tastes the sculpted black skeletons of billion-year-old gneiss.

The ashes swirled dry and gray on the surface of the water for a few moments. Then they were gone.

It's been a wet winter along the rim of the Grand Canyon and snow is moving through the rock. A uranium mine six miles from the hub of the nation's second most visited national park is being expanded. A new shaft cuts down into the sandstone but the mining hasn't yet begun. Water runs through the rock and the shaft fills. Work is slowed until pumps are flicked on and the snowmelt is brought back to the surface. It is sprayed into a containment pond from sprinklers that hang in the wind. A Diné activist who in years past was repeatedly handcuffed to keep treated wastewater from being turned to artificial snow for ski slopes on sacred mountains, wears a bandana over his face and arrives at the gates of the mine. When he asks questions, the company says the sprinklers are nothing to worry about. The activist paces through the national forest land outside the compound fence and captures photos of the mist that sails into the ponderosa pine. When the mist is later tested, it's found to exceed EPA uranium limits for drinking water.

Phil Lyman doesn't want to lose the war. His supporters write letters to the local newspaper about a secret plan to make national parks everywhere in order to force the people off the land and into the cities, or maybe even camps. Guns are stockpiled. But their candidate, Trump, the real-estate baron who only goes outside to golf and who never speaks about public lands or national parks, wins. Many in Utah said he was too cruel, too much like the men who drove the Mormons east from New York to Missouri to Illinois to Deseret. But Phil Lyman sees a break in the onslaught. In the days after the election, he writes that it is time to get rid of "our sworn enemies the environmentalists." He sees work ahead. "I don't know if we can get rid of the neo-environmentalist parasites, but maybe we can get them the heck out of Utah."

We keep arriving. Parasites who produce nothing. Who don't want to gather our own firewood but complain about the drill rigs going in. Who pretend beef comes from supermarkets and that hummus is food. Who talk about the changing climate but who always seem to be driving or flying off to exotic vacations. Who leech and leech and work at keyboards and keep growing in numbers with each attack against us like coyotes. Who imagine ourselves as allied with the Native American communities even as we move in and crowd the homeland as so many others have before.

A respected Ute Mountain Ute elder carried the flag at the front of the procession for five miles. He'd been ousted from the tribal council for asking the last US president to create the lines of a national monument around the graves of his foremothers and forefathers. He looks at the dry earth being carried by the wind and thinks of what's underground. "Water is life. From day one, I've mentioned that," he says. "This land is a way of life for us as human beings." He says the uranium mill was constructed on the graves of his people, that the fences of the mill block Ute hunting routes. The place, he says, is sacred and powerful. The ancients have not left.

"I saw a vision as we were walking," he tells me. "It was a calmness, a whisper in the wind. I could hear the ancestors were with us."

It's after the protest, after the public hearing. The state will renew the mill license. The trucks will keep rolling. The parasites will keep leeching and will not be exterminated. I need to orient myself. I walk out my front door and down into the floodplain of the San Juan River—a tributary of the Colorado. I can see the stone warrior lying on the eastern horizon. He's pasted black against the clouds which are just starting to glow in the evening light. His eyes, nose, chin, and the great mound of his arms on his chest are so distinct against the sky, he seems ready to spring up and take to the battle again.

I walk for fifteen minutes until I'm standing beside the brown waters of the San Juan. Crouching on the bank, I plunge a hand beneath the surface. My head is bowed toward my knees, my toes just staying dry, and as my eyes slide shut, I reach out with fingertips to see in the dark. The current presses past, lifting my hand with its pulse.

This is how I remember where I am and how I got here. I reach into the rolling San Juan and imagine my way downstream through the canyons where no road follows. I feel where the water cuts through a ridge of sandstone and into domes of ancient seabed. This was the first river I floated, my car seat strapped to the wooden deck of an army surplus raft when I was fourteen months old, my mother carrying me around even the small rapids. For miles the San Juan sparkles around graceful bends that canyon walls have been instructed to follow. Reaching farther, the current slackens, the mud and sand and uranium in its waters sifting back to the riverbed. The river pours over a sloped, sliding waterfall and halts in the clear dead waters of Lake Powell. Where jetboats rip down the main channel, I turn right and press on. When the current begins to move again beyond the borders of the reservoir, I'm in a new river, the Colorado, and I head upstream through the explosive whitewater of Cataract Canyon, past Satan's Gut, and slide through the confluence of the Green River. I move through lazy golden waters and across the valley that holds the town of Moab, then on into another carmine-red canyon burnished with a black patina where my parents scattered Steve's ashes twenty-five years ago. I reach past the arched scaffolding of an old wooden bridge destroyed by a tourist's wayward campfire a few years back. From the remnants of its deck sway a few chunks of charcoal.

Just beyond, the river splits. Both canyons take me home. Right goes to the Dolores River, the crazy meanders of rose-colored canyons lined with sage and Mormon tea then piñon and juniper then, as you move higher, ponderosa pine. Most years that river is a limpid creek, choked off from its headwaters by six million cubic yards of rock, gravel, and sand pressed into a 270-foot-tall plug. Beyond is the place where my parents built their yurt. I go left after the burned bridge, passing through Westwater Canyon before crossing the Colorado state line and the beach where we scattered my mother's ashes. I don't stop until I've gone through the heart of a city, another canyon, the grassy banks of ranchlands pocked with fracking wells and up two right turns on smaller tributaries. I've reached the creek that rumbles past my childhood home. Years ago, I would sit by its waters carving sticks into the semblance of whitewater kayaks and sending them through deadly, six-inch-high Niagaras. I'd watch them disappear around the corner, curious where they'd end up. Now after months and years of living out of kayaks and rafts, I've paddled every mile of river from the mouth of that creek to the sea. I've paddled the Dolores from the dam and the San Juan from my house to where both rivers meet the Colorado. I've seen how this landscape is sewn together by water. And now

I've come to rest on the banks of a river in Utah where locals tell me I'll never belong.

I pull my hand dripping from the San Juan and stand on the beach with stiff legs. My movement startles a flock of Canada geese that had walked up on a sandbar while I was crouched motionless. They lumber into the air, honking and annoyed.

Flowing far beneath my feet are underground tributaries I'll never trace. A massive, slow-flowing aquifer creeps under this beach, adding to the flow of the San Juan as it passes from southern Utah toward Arizona. Our town's well taps into that aquifer. As does the well that feeds the Ute village to the north. And above it all rests the White Mesa Uranium Mill.

My mother was fifty-two years old when she died. Even this is a long time for a life of the flesh, as Prisllena Rabbit knows. Long enough to understand patterns, to plant tomatoes or float rivers year after year, to begin to learn respect. Our memories can stretch longer, the river that brought my parents home, the trail that delivered the pioneers across the plateaus, the warrior mountain that sleeps until he is needed. These stories will be forgotten. But the trucks that rumble down the highways carry something more patient, elements that in five swift ticks of decay recall the age of the planet; uranium-238 has a half-life of 4.5 billion years. These elements bear our prodding and may submit to their burials, but only for a period of time that a long animal life can be tricked into believing is relevant. The burials are on the move. When they mix into the slow underground rivers and find their way out into once-sacred springs, new stories will arise. Stories about waters that kill. Dangerous powers that were pulled from the earth, tampered with, and forced back into the ground. The curiosity that opened the pouch could not be reversed. The enemies of the people escaped. Spirits of powerful stones wander in the homeland.

The warrior sleeps, the stars shine cold and close. The heron stabs at lizards on the riverbank. As our bones go into the ground, as our dust blows across the land—that, maybe, is how we begin to belong.

*A*ll day he walks ahead of me, his body lithe and his feet sure as he skirts the canyon's edge. At times juniper branches grab onto my pack, but they never seem to touch his. He's spent five decades in the desert, and his bag is as much a part of him as the top of his head or the width of his shoulders.

Anywhere that can be hiked in a day is merely training, he tells me; anywhere that can be reached by a trail is for the tourists. The goal is to find a place where you can ask this question: How many centuries have passed since someone else stood here?

This landscape is alive with ancient traces—pictographs, cliff dwellings, arrowheads. He points to a crack running down a boulder like a lightning bolt and says, There's a painted pot in there.

I believe him. He is seventy-one. Together we've lived exactly one hundred years.

We hike for nine hours straight the first day and in that time he never stops talking—wild, ranging conversations and soliloquies and rants. He speaks of his past, local politics, the battles for Utah wilderness. He reads the fortune of our doomed town and our doomed state and our doomed planet, and explains that nothing is ever truly doomed. Tales flow from the years he has spent camping and hiking alone. Snooping, he calls it.

Again and again he takes a stand—controversial, untenable—and holds it against all my objections until I relent and he is free to walk out the line of his own reasoning. He lets his argument guide him in a great arcing loop until everything he'd first claimed is knocked on its side. When he returns to where he started, he is holding some new view with as much conviction as the first. Early in the day I'd pointed this out, but I soon realized to talk oneself in circles was exercise. Koans stretched across miles of slickrock. The point of a walk is to return to your door transformed, not hardened in your habits. Hikes to keep the body strong and paradoxes to keep the mind from growing complacent.

In nine hours, we pause only to down a fistful of peanuts and to refill our water jugs in a hidden spring.

He was once a poet and he recites lines to the moment. We've hauled our packs up a tongue of slickrock and are standing on a high, wide ledge with a view for a hundred miles, when it's Carolyn Forché:

You live
like a brief wisp
in a giant place.

Years ago he walked away from a career or two to come here and walk. He left a marriage in the city to live closer to the canyons. The daughters he helped raise will hardly talk to him anymore. Now it's feet to the ground every day.

What can the old hope for? he asks, quoting a question once posed to an Australian aboriginal elder in a book. Strong legs, the man had answered.

He then recites a few lines he wrote thirty years before:

I am learning to be an old man
It's slow work
I am taking my time

*Every winter, he goes south to spend months among the sa-
guaros, and he hikes both sides of the border fence. Once, he came
across two bales of marijuana lying in the American cactus—
packed into tight green blocks and dropped on the run. He buried
them for later.*

*This year he found a skull, a human skull, clean and white as
paper in the moonlight. Two dark caverns of eye sockets guarded
a little shade where a man's memories once rode. Teeth lined the
jaw. There were no ribs or femurs or vertebrae, just the skull. The
ranger he notified told him this was not the thirst-driven death of
a migrant; this was a message, a marking of territory. Like a dog
pissing on a telephone pole. He shows me a picture on his phone.*

*In nine hours, his pace never slows, but as the winter light
sinks into the afternoon rock his boots begin to scrape across ledges
as we move uphill. It is as if he has to pause for them to catch up
as one might pause for an old hound scrambling up a steep slope
behind.*

*We walk through the sunset while he searches for the perfect
campsite. He wants it to face east toward the rising sun. He insists
it have a sandstone wall so he can wake up in his sleeping bag and
lean against the wall while he drinks coffee in the first warm light.
We never find the right spot. He worries we'll run out of water
tomorrow.*

*There are more days like this, but a week later, I'm in the can-
yons alone. I return and find the painted pot tucked in its hiding
place. It is a seed jar, orange with red paint, and it's at least eight
hundred years old. I think of the thousands of artifacts that have
disappeared from this mesa. I sense the destruction creeping across
the land even as I crouch in the quiet sunlight before the perfect
pot.*

*Leaving the jar where it belongs, I sit with a notebook. Koans,
desert, doomed. Pen touches page and twenty words pour out for
my friend with the strong legs:*

Still walking ahead
The zen curmudgeon
Offers slickrock syllogisms
To the fading light—
We're fucked, he says.
Isn't it beautiful?

(2017)

THE DELTA

Spring 2014

I stepped into line at the Hollow Mountain gas station in Hanksville, Utah (population 215), holding an overpriced string cheese. Three or four sunburnt customers stood in front of me with Fritos and fountain drinks, waiting for the cashier to finish a tirade he was delivering to the man across the counter. The cashier's voice boomed off the windowless walls of the store that sits fully inside a blasted-out sandstone cliff, the "hollow mountain" tourist hole frequented by houseboaters headed to Lake Powell and desert rats hoping to get lost in canyon country.

The speech sounded political. "Obama comes down here . . . government . . . thinking they can run the place . . ."

I waited it out with my string cheese.

Lurid colors oozed from racks of magazines. I tended to an itch on the back of my head and felt something hard in a tangle of hair. Working it loose, I discovered a small black feather.

". . . bureaucrats out in Washington . . ."

For four days, I'd been living in sandstone slot canyons, tortuous openings in the earth sculpted smooth by centuries of rain. Utah had always been a place to escape for me, and wedging myself into the slots fifty feet off the ground—feet against one wall, back against the other—had always felt like freedom.

But not now. My mom had died after a four-month battle with cancer five weeks earlier. I came here to meet friends and get out of the house where I'd lived with my dad, sister, and girlfriend for my mom's last few months. I came searching for open space, silence, rock, but the day before, I'd panicked in the canyons. The walls became a cage. My body was both rigid and weak. I froze, unable to go forward or back, my right leg bobbing uncontrollably as if to a frenzied, arrhythmic drumbeat. There had been little rain that spring. The potholes at the bottoms of the slots were all dry, and I sat shaking above the red mud lines where the water once ran.

When I made it back to the cars, I told my friends they could go find more canyons without me. They left me with a hug and a hand-rolled joint. I smoked the latter that night, and as I lay in my sleeping bag, my eyes dried against the desert air. The guttural groans of toads wallowing in a nearby stock tank hammered into my skull. The walls closed in again.

I dreamed the same dream I'd been having for weeks. The light was golden with fall as I stood on the shore of a river waiting for something. Overhead, the cottonwood branches blazed with yellow leaves. My mom was dead and gone, and I was there to face that fact. But just as I was sinking into my sorrow, she came around the bend, rowing a gray raft and smiling at me from beneath a straw hat. Each night, at this moment, I'd fail to wave back. I'd turn away and walk upslope until the river was out of sight. If she was still alive, I didn't want to know. I couldn't face her.

Morning broke. Sometime in the night, the toad chorus coming through the hood of my sleeping bag had been replaced by the moans of cattle. I felt no relief even as the sun climbed across the great sandstone fins of the San Rafael Swell. Fresh wet patties lay across the road, buzzing with greenish flies. I packed up and went to town.

The line at the gas station still hadn't budged.

"Out in Washington, they think they can do what they want. But do they even know? Ranches are drying up. Lake Powell is shrinking."

Water talk? I wondered.

"People are losing jobs," the man continued. "There's a scam up and down the Colorado River."

I'd lived on that river for eight months in the last two years, paddling from its two highest sources in Colorado and Wyoming all the way to the ocean. Now I listened intently.

"We're in the middle of a drought. The reservoirs are all disappearing down in California, and do you know what they're doing? They're dumping water onto the Mexican desert. Say it's for the birds. What a waste."

The customer across the counter, red-eyed and holding an unopened Monster energy drink, rose out of a slouch. He sensed the lecture coming to an end and nodded.

"Now, either they're all idiots," the cashier emphasized each word as he laid out the last bit of proof, "or there's something downright diabolical going on."

Farms and cities were phantoms to me, the lost jobs the man spoke of were speculation. But I could picture that water spilling into the desert. I'd seen photos of it a few days before. The release was taking place south of the border in the swaths of sand and weeds where the Colorado River goes to die. For the first time since the Colorado dried up in the 1960s, water was being released into its former delta. I'd crossed the delta by foot a couple of years earlier on my source-to-sea trip, and it was one of the least pleasant walks I'd ever taken—a mess of trash, cracked mud, and brutal sun. I had never planned to return. But now, over a thousand miles from that place, the river called. I needed flowing water, not dry canyons.

With the cashier's speech finished, the line moved forward. Over the counter, I handed a dollar bill and a few coins without a word.

I got in my car and sat with the key unturned in the ignition. Maps were strewn across the passenger seat. In the back, a climbing rope lay tangled around my sleeping pad and a five-gallon jug. My mobile apartment. In the fall, I'd abandoned a grad school philosophy program to move back in with my family after my mom was diagnosed. Now she was gone, and I was between everything. I had no prospects for employment. My bank account was in the low triple digits, but what was I doing here alone when water was flowing across the Colorado Delta again?

The cashier's words reverberated through the car. *He is right*, I thought. The water *is* being wasted, at least according to the basic economic vision we're bombarded with daily—investment should lead to payoff. His outrage seemed concordant with some deep-seated parts of our culture: there is nothing more sacrilegious to our economic order than expenditure without return; nothing that cuts against common sense more than use without productivity; nothing more demonic, more diabolical, than waste.

I sat at the intersection next to the gas station pondering my options. Right took me to more canyons. To my left, many miles and dollars down the road, was Mexico.

I turned the wheel.

If you travel to the highest source of the Colorado River basin at the headwaters of the Green River in Wyoming and start downstream, you'll see more or less what you'd expect: a waterway that grows in volume as it flows downhill. Up where the Green begins in the rocky, grizzly-studded Wind River Mountains, you'll find a creek—farther down, a river. And farther still, if you appear during peak runoff or during a flash flood, you might catch a glimpse of the frothing behemoth that carved the Grand Canyon. Water still explodes in cataracts rafters call "whitewater," but the river was more properly named by the Spaniards, *Colorado*, the colored-red river. A mouthful will leave you chewing on the grit of waterborne sandstone for hours.

For over a thousand miles, the river does what rivers do, starts small and grows. Sure, there are a few man-made hiccups along the way (if you can call the nation's two largest reservoirs "hiccups"), but for the most part the river picks up more volume as it moves toward the sea. But it never arrives. Somewhere around Las Vegas and the Hoover Dam, the Colorado flows through a funhouse mirror of modernity and the process reverses. Where the tributaries upstream fed the Colorado through meandering canyons, now they drain its waters away in straight-line canals. The water that poured into the growing river now leaves to feed the Southwest's ever-growing cities. All the way down at the border, after a long series of reservoirs and diversions, the Morelos Dam funnels the remaining water from the riverbed into a final concrete canal. Not a drop is left unclaimed. Fifty years without steady water, and you can hear Colorado's delta below—once three thousand square miles of diverse wetlands, lagoons, pools, and labyrinthine channels—gasp, let out a dry death-rattle of despair, and croak. Almost.

March 23, 2014. The window-like penstocks of the Morelos Dam straddling the US-Mexico border were cranked open for the first time in decades. Water crept forward and edged out across sand. It ran, pooled, ran again, remembering its old course. Teams of scientists, members of environmental groups, and politicians stood on the banks—they posed for photographs and lined up to give speeches under the glaring sun.

The flood worked its way forward. Press coverage showed locals coming out to see their long-vanished river. Friends called friends and soon a crowd gathered. Truck speakers rocked with the horn-driven bounce of *norteño* music. Children splashed in the cool water. Somebody started selling ice cream.

Over fifteen years of work by environmental groups on both sides of the border had led to this historic agreement between the governments of the United States and Mexico. Historic because for the first time, water was being dumped in the delta—not out of necessity like in rare years of excess nor as a way to dispose of water too saline for further agricultural use—but deliberately, and at least according to the gas station cashier, for no good reason. Up until then, the river's entire flow with few exceptions was captured, stored, and parceled out toward various "beneficial uses," be they municipal, industrial, or agricultural. The benefit was profit. But on that March day and for the next two months until the release was scheduled to end, there was no hope of return, no profit, no payout.

Wasted. In the West, water is money. And the thirsty Mexican sand was sucking up money like executive bonuses at a failing bank. Each drop of water that sank into the sand, ran out of a child's hair, or fed a seedling cottonwood would never irrigate a cash crop or turn a water meter. And—who could say?—some might even be lost to the sea. Talk about diabolical.

Getting to Mexico took longer than I expected. I posted up at my girlfriend's house where I sent emails to every kayaker I knew, asking if they wanted to paddle across the overgrown weed farm that is the Colorado's delta. I managed to track down several willing paddlers—including a magazine editor and a videographer—who were planning to give it a trial run. By the time we had it all arranged, it was close to a month after water had begun to flow in the delta. We agreed to meet near the border as soon as possible. We'd cross the delta together—or we'd try, at least.

I warned them that it wouldn't be easy. My only other experience in the delta came at the end of a 2012 paddling trip that took me 1,700 miles down the length of the Green and

Colorado Rivers. My companion and I rode small, inflatable packrafts down ever-shrinking concrete channels designed to distribute irrigation water along the border between the states of Baja Norte and Sonora in northern Mexico. A few times per hour, we'd run into a diversion structure or low-head dam and we'd have to portage. We'd get back in the water, pungent with sewage and decorated with plastic pop bottles, and keep floating.

One evening, we were having trouble finding a place to camp and a truckload of tough, swaggering teenagers stopped beside the canal. They told us in fluent English we needed to get out of the water so they could "inspect our bags for stolen stuff." We demurred. They told us we needed to exit the canal because there was a big rapid downstream . . . and some corrupt security guards . . . and that the police were on their way . . . and so on for thirty minutes. Physically dragging us from the ditch would have meant wading in the sewage water up past their knee-length jerseys and fancily stitched jeans. They eventually left and we hid our packrafts under a pile of trash on the side of the canal. We jogged a half-mile away into a farm field, crawled into a patch of brush, and waited out the night.

The water ran out completely on our fifth day in the canal, and we began to bushwhack. The dense thickets of tamarisk, an invasive Eurasian species, required a painstaking crawl to get through. For two days, we moved so slowly that Tai Chi classes and DMV lines would have appeared rushed in comparison. When the brush cleared, we dragged ourselves across expansive mudflats to the sea.

The delta was once a very different place. For roughly six million years the Colorado filtered its way to the Gulf of California, not as a channelized river, but as a diverse oasis sprawling out over two million acres. Early Spanish explorers found crossing the complicated wetland jungle more foreboding than traversing the hundreds of miles of desert that surrounded it in every other direction. When naturalist Aldo Leopold canoed across the delta in 1922, he reported finding "a hundred miles of lovely desolation," a natural bird sanctuary where the river "was nowhere and everywhere" because it could not decide which of a thousand passages offered "the most pleasant and least speedy path to the Gulf."

In less than a century, the river was more nowhere than everywhere. By 2012, only 10 percent of its original wetlands were still wet. The other 90 percent had been converted to farmlands or had dried into sandy monocultures of tamarisk. Most of the remaining habitat was in La Ciénega de Santa Clara, *ciénega* meaning marshland, which was formed accidentally in the 1970s after Mexican farmers noted that the water being transported across the US border was too saline for farming and was in violation of a treaty agreement. The American government built a canal to capture salty agricultural runoff in southern Arizona and sent it sixty miles across the former delta. Construction crews never finished the project, and the canal ended abruptly in the middle of the desert. Water spilled out onto flats, far from any town, and within a couple of decades forty thousand acres of wetlands had reappeared. The accidental marsh now supports 280 species of birds, and every winter roughly three hundred thousand migratory birds flock to La Ciénega.

To the west, the Rio Hardy—another smaller wetland created by agricultural runoff on the Mexican side of the border—also supports diverse birdlife. But for the most part, the delta provides habitat only for cultivated iceberg lettuce and other invasive plants. The Gulf of California, no longer infused with freshwater from the Colorado, has lost dozens of species and its once-productive fisheries have collapsed.

Ecologists I met during my source-to-sea trip explained that with just 1 percent of the Colorado's average annual flow dedicated to restoration in the delta, the river would reconnect with the sea, greatly expanding the wildlife habitat and rejuvenating the estuary in the process. And in 2012, the governments north and south of the border decided to give it a shot. Minute 319 was added to the 1944 treaty that grants Mexico roughly one-tenth of the Colorado River's average flow, or in water manager terms, 1.5 million acre-feet. All of Mexico's allotted water is put to use on farmlands and none is reserved for environmental flows. The new amendment allowed Mexico to store their share of the water in US reservoirs during surplus years and it allowed the US to send less water to Mexico during droughts. It also laid the groundwork for the "pulse flow," a release of 105,000 acre-feet of water, donated by the US, Mexico, and nonprofit groups, to the riverbed.

I met Jeff and Todd, two Americans from a paddling magazine, in Southern California, and we crossed the border just after dawn on a mid-April morning. The pulse flow had been underway for a month, but the water table was still filling up and the river had yet to connect with the ocean. I was ready to finish my source-to-sea trip, by boat this time, not on foot. But my motivation was also philosophical, catalyzed by the comment I overheard in the Utah gas station and the work of an obscure French surrealist, a pornographic novelist turned philosopher, named Georges Bataille. I wanted to see waste in action, and Bataille filled bookshelves with his analyses of waste.

Two years earlier, as I was paddling to the still-waterless delta by kayak, I uncovered a five-gallon bucket of food we'd stashed near Lake Mead before our trip. Alongside Snickers bars, turkey jerky, and a few twenty-four-ounce cans of Busch beer, I'd packed *The Accursed Share, Volume I*, Bataille's 1949 treatise on economics where he introduces the concept of "general economy." I read it in the following weeks while paddling down the increasingly industrialized lower Colorado River. The book became as redolent as the smell of burnt Folgers coffee, which always transports me to my grandfather's house in rural Illinois. In the same way, the vast systems of storage, irrigation, and pipelines that drain the lower Colorado became tied in my mind to Bataille's not entirely sane ramblings. Now that I was returning to the delta, his ideas came rushing back. As we bumped down the pothole-ridden streets on our way to the river, I tried to recall the outlines of the Frenchman's economic theory.

According to Bataille, any understanding we have of economics that concentrates on growth and wealth is limited in scope. Given a larger lens, it becomes apparent that waste, or sacrifice, plays as important a role as production in defining how a system operates.

"I will begin with a basic fact," says Bataille in the opening pages of this three-volume work on general economy. "The living organism, in a situation determined by the play of energy on the surface of the globe, ordinarily receives more energy than is necessary for maintaining life." The excess, he says, is used for growth. For example, sunlight hits a plant, photosynthesis occurs, the plant grows bigger, produces more leaves, absorbs more sunlight, and grows more quickly. So far so good. But then comes Bataille's kicker, radical in its obviousness: "If the system can no longer grow, or if the excess cannot be completely absorbed in its growth, it must necessarily be lost without profit; it must be spent, willingly or not, gloriously or catastrophically." And Bataille is soon arguing that this simple equation applies equally to plant life and to the global economic order.

Bataille could be called a critic of productivity, but he is also—and perhaps even more so—a proponent of waste. While so many well-worn arguments have been made against the onslaught of production (that it has dissevered us from nature; that it's causing us to outrun our own limits; that it's overindulgent; that we need to restrain, discipline, control ourselves instead of trying to control nature), Bataille enters from the other side. "*It is not necessity,*" he emphasizes, "*but its contrary, 'luxury,' that presents living matter and mankind with their fundamental problems.*" Flipping the standard economic principles that scarcity and utility drive systems of exchange, Bataille argues the central factor of economics is how we deal with surplus. Today, for the most part, we turn surplus back into more profit. Capitalists reinvest capital in capitalism.

But Bataille reminds us that hasn't always been the case. Most non-capitalist societies built entire religious systems around sacrifice, erected huge non-utilitarian monuments, or sunk resources into nonproductive monastic life. (One of many examples Bataille gives is from Tibet in the early twentieth century where, according to one scholar's estimates, the total budget of the monastic system in the country "would have been twice as large as that of the [entire government], eight times that of the army.") Contrast this with postindustrial capitalism where we've attempted to optimize everything toward profit and return. In the Colorado River system, for example, it's estimated that each drop of water is reused (profitably) *seventeen times*. While we've gone further than any other culture before us in manipulating the planet toward productive ends, nonproductive expenditure still forces itself upon us as much as ever, be it in economic or ecological collapse, or in sudden eruptions of violence.

The global movement of energy "cannot accumulate limitlessly in productive forces," Bataille writes. "Eventually, like a river to the sea, it is bound to escape us and be lost." His crucial point is that we can *either* be stewards of waste—that is, we can find less volatile ways to burn off surplus wealth that can't be made productive—*or* we can be its victims. Bataille claims that excess wealth always threatens to destabilize the system. To maintain stability, he thinks the surplus can be spent on nonproductive arts and cultural life (think Tibetan monasteries), lavish spectacle (think NFL games and Burning Man), or in the public sphere (think universal healthcare and national parks).

Yet so much political discourse today revolves around growth, jobs, *the* economy. In our quest to produce, we've almost forgotten how to waste. There are exceptions, however, such as taking 105,000 acre-feet of perfectly good water and letting it drain into the desert.

On the Mexico side of the border, we joined two locals, Jorge, a professor of hydrology, and Victor, a sea kayak guide from Baja, who also wanted to check out the grand experiment in the delta. They directed us to follow their car.

We drove south together for forty-five minutes, and turned onto a trash-lined dirt road. Jorge led us through a maze of unmarked intersections so complicated that I don't think I could have found my way back out. Several times, we plowed into sand pits, the wheels on Jorge's passenger car spinning to get through. We crested a rise and saw the river slipping through a row of sand-choked culverts: clear, swirling water.

As we loaded our boats, looked over maps, and prepared to launch, I chatted with the two Mexicans in our party, both of whom had built their lives around water in the state of Baja Norte where the only perennial river (the Colorado) is no longer perennial. Though Victor had spent much of his life in the seat of a kayak, honing his skills in the technical ocean rock gardens near his home in Ensenada, this would be his first time paddling a river. Jorge, a professor at the Universidad Autonoma de Baja California in Mexicali, told me he had been monitoring groundwater in the delta of the Rio Colorado for thirty years. He'd never paddled a canoe before.

Jorge muttered something about *narcotraficantes* when a shiny SUV ripped past us on the remote dirt road. The word was enough to speed up our final preparations. We'd heard rumors of cartel airstrips hidden in the delta brush that Jorge wouldn't confirm or deny. In twenty minutes, we were floating.

Soon enough, drug running was no longer on our minds. We paddled down a channel that had been bulldozed razor-straight to make way for the pulse flow. Victor explored side channels in his sea kayak while Jeff taught Jorge, his bowman, various canoeing strokes. Below us were the waving tops of small tamarisk trees. A month ago, the trees were relying on taproots that grow up to one hundred feet to reach evasive desert water. Now fish, riding the pulse flow south, darted in and out of the eddies formed by their branches.

Water law in the western US, for all its complications, is often distilled down into two simple catchphrases: "First in time, first in right" and "Use it or lose it." Settlers who arrived in the West early on and diverted a river or creek to a legally recognized "beneficial use" locked in priority rights on that water. During water shortages, those with the oldest water rights can force junior water users upstream to turn off their irrigation canals. But even today you have to prove you're actively using your water right if you want to keep it valid. If you're caught wasting any of the water you're entitled to (by leaving it in the stream, for example), your right may be permanently forfeited, and everyone else moves up a notch on the priority list.

With these parameters in mind and the great arid expanse of the West ripe for the stealing (few ever stopped to ask the indigenous residents), nineteenth-century settlers got to using. They diverted, irrigated, and dammed with an increasing intensity until every drop of water in the Colorado was "benefited" from. Today, people from Phoenix to Las Vegas, from Los Angeles to Denver, get at least some of their drinking water from the Colorado River, and it irrigates fresh produce that is shipped around the country each winter.

While good for profit, the legal system doesn't come without conflict. How well it works is captured by a bit of wisdom attributed to Mark Twain: "Whiskey's for drinkin, water's for fightin."

If Georges Bataille could have been convinced to care about water in the West, he probably would have been skeptical about a system that doesn't allow for intentional waste—or as he liked to call it, sacrifice. Bataille was obsessed with sacrifice. The human sacrifice of the Aztecs especially fascinated him—the beautiful young men dragged to the top of pyramids so their still-beating hearts could be sliced out with obsidian blades to feed the blood-thirsty sun. But he was also intrigued by the animal and ritual sacrifices around which countless cultures built their religious lives. What impulse, Bataille asked, drove people, after a long season of backbreaking labor, to destroy their best ram, their largest bull? Why would farmers take a crop of corn and let it rot into the ground or go up in flames? Why waste what you've worked so hard to produce? The standard interpretation today is that, in a naïve attempt to appease the gods that controlled their fate, "primitive" people convinced themselves they needed to sacrifice their most valuable possessions in order to propitiate the deities. If you believe your survival depends on pleasing the powers that be, then it's no mystery why you'd be willing to give up some of your prize surplus in order to satisfy those powers. Laying a lamb on the altar was, therefore, an investment: sacrifice now and expect rewards later.

This pseudo-capitalist line of thinking, says Bataille, gets it exactly backwards. He argues the sacrifice is not done to get a bigger return next year but to feel sovereign over the cycle of work that produced the sacrificial offering. All year, the farmer has been storing surplus, which Bataille claims makes him "not a man [but the] plow of the one who eats the bread." But at the moment of sacrifice, the farmer, for a brief moment, ceases being a servant of accumulation and saving; he or she breaks the cycle by destroying something of value. The goal of ancient rituals was not primarily to please the gods in hope of some future return, Bataille claims, but to be present among the gods at the moment of ceremonial waste.

At the end of the engineered channel, sacrificial water poured into the brush, inches deep and warming quickly in the sun.

The delta had been riverless for so long that without man-made banks to hold it in, the water was lost, spilling across the flats. Our paddles became ineffective and we pulled ourselves forward on plants, watching out for the limbs of thorny mesquite trees. The current slowed until we could no longer tell if the water was flowing. The GPS came out. Jorge concluded we must keep bearing south by southeast to find the Rio Hardy, a permanent channel of agricultural runoff that occasionally spills into the sea during the highest of high tides. Jorge told us that if the water from the pulse flow made it to the Rio Hardy, the Colorado would have officially reconnected, however briefly, with salt water.

We kept pulling ourselves around stands of brush, unable to move in a straight line. Another group of paddlers had made the same crossing the week before and gave us some pointers. "Turn left at the Red Ant Tree," one of them had written in an email. We weren't sure if such a marker would be easy to find in the labyrinth. Soon enough, though, a lone cottonwood appeared, an apparition of electric green in the swamps of grayish tamarisk. As I paddled closer, the trunk looked odd. It was shimmering as if battling unstable heat waves or a reddish static. The entire base of the tree was alive, swarming with a stranded colony of fire ants that had been forced out of the ground by the first substantial flood in years. The insects paced up and down with that collective urgency of ant panic. They must have been stranded for well over a week.

We followed the channel to the left, and the river began to disappear before our eyes. Shallow sandbars forced us to get out and drag our boats, and before long we were wading through ankle-deep puddles.

"The Rio Hardy is three hundred meters away," Jorge said, looking at his GPS. The tamarisk in front of us had thickened into a wall and there was no visible way through.

"You head that way," Victor told me with a nod to the south. "I'll climb that tree and see if I can get a view." There were no landmarks visible on the horizon, and the dead branches of what was once a cottonwood offered the only hope at gaining a vantage point.

I ventured off in the direction Victor suggested, pushed into the brush, and caught a glimmer of water beyond the branches. I cut back toward the group and could hear their voices clearly through a tangled thicket. Crashing toward them, I was back in the delta I remembered from my first trip. The branches were so tightly knit I was almost suspended off the ground, unable to move in any direction. I tried crawling. I tried climbing over the top, only to fall into the middle of a tree, leaving my arms and legs streaked with bloody scratches. The air in the brush was humid and heavy. Black dust stuck to the sweat on my face. The only thing that worked was to break down each skinny branch by hand, moving forward at a couple of feet per minute. Victor, back with the group via another route, began slamming his kayak into the brush from the other side. Eventually we met. Using the boat as a battering ram, we bashed our way through the last sixty meters to the Rio Hardy. It had taken us five hours to cover about a mile and a quarter.

Exhausted and bleeding, we regrouped on the water. Jorge, otherwise reserved and quite possibly traumatized from his introduction to canoeing, called our attention to a small waterfall spilling into the deeper Rio Hardy channel. His voice trembled with emotion. He'd been tracking the movement of the pulse flow since it began and knew better than anybody how the water was behaving. There was a 10 percent margin of error in his team's measurement stations upstream and downstream from where we sat, he explained. Since the water from the Morelos Dam release was less than 10 percent of the total flow of the Hardy, there was no way for the hydrologists to tell for certain whether the river water had reconnected with the sea.

What we were witnessing deep in the tamarisk jungle was water from the pulse flow dumping into the Rio Hardy. From there, it would spill over into the ocean at the next full moon tide. The pulse flow would never amount to a continuous above-ground connection between the Gulf of California and the Colorado River; the depleted water table upstream from where we started paddling had forced the release underground for at least a dozen miles. But the murmuring spout of water around which we'd gathered, not much larger than flow from a fountain in a city park, was the Colorado River on its way to mix with the sea for the first time in over a decade.

"The rivers are communicating," Jorge announced.

We made camp as night fell. The swamp hummed with the constant chatter of birdsong. Jeff lit a fire, and I relaxed onto the warm ground. After my winter in Colorado trapped in the echoing halls of cancer talk—late-night Google searches for whether Cisplatin treatment is effective for those with K-RAS genotypes and what clinical trials were available in Minnesota or Pennsylvania—I'd landed back on the earth again. It felt good to move, to paddle, to sit in the dirt. My mom taught me over many years of river trips together that paddling allows for a less dramatic version of Bataille's sacrifice: simply soaking in moments with no desire for future rewards.

Walking was the preferred method used by another eccentric philosopher who succumbed to tuberculosis one hundred years before Bataille lay down on his deathbed in 1962. Henry David Thoreau, pioneer of the neckbeard, was seeking something that aligns with Bataille's notion of sacrifice—a wasted life.

I once spent three weeks on a college philosophy project, part of which required me to read *Walden*. I'd read the first and longest chapter, "Economy," a couple of times in high school, but I couldn't keep my eyes open in the book's second half where Thoreau drones on about winter animals and the pond. I was going to read the whole thing this time, I promised myself, but again I found "Economy" the most interesting section. I still remember my professor's feedback when I turned in my paper. "Did you read the second half of the book?" he asked. I'd failed again.

In those first hundred pages, Thoreau offers a careful accounting of life's necessities. His goal is to flip the ratio of work and leisure common in antebellum America (six days on, one Sabbath off) to its opposite (one day on, six Sabbaths off). We remember Thoreau for his refusal to pay his poll tax that was going to be used to fund the Mexican-American War, the conflict during which the US stole much of the Colorado River basin from Mexico. But equally revolutionary was Thoreau's mission to prove that you could opt out of the cycle of debt, saving, and spending that so many of his countrymen were trapped in. "It may be guessed," Thoreau asserts early in *Walden*, "that I reduce almost the whole advantage of holding this superfluous property as a fund in store against the future, so far as the individual is concerned, mainly to the defraying of funeral expenses." Only later, when I read Bataille, did I realize that Thoreau's economics were a manual for wasting time, for sacrificing our future on the beauty and immensity of the present.

Could this method be compared to the ritual slaughters of old? In the modern world where wealth is measured in hours worked and dollars earned, not head of sheep, perhaps time is one of our most valuable possessions. Ben Franklin's "Advice to a Young Tradesman" sums up the nature of time under capitalism in precise terms. "Remember that time is money," writes Franklin to an imaginary young entrepreneur. If you take the afternoon off from work and spend a little money on entertainment, Franklin scolds, you've not only wasted the spending money but also the half-day you could have been working. But that's not all.

Remember that money is of the prolific, generating nature. Money can beget money, and its offspring can beget more, and so on . . . The more there is of it, the more it produces at every turning, so that the profits rise quicker and quicker . . .

In short, the way to wealth, if you desire it, is plain as the way to market. It depends chiefly on two words, industry and frugality; that is, waste neither time nor money, but make the best use of both.

Compare that mentality to the life Thoreau idealized: frittering away his youth beside Walden Pond in an alternative type of unpaid internship. Thoreau's method of accounting becomes the frontline of resistance against Franklin's pervasive logic. Forget the slaughtering of scapegoats; under capitalism, intentional loafing amounts to ceremonial sacrifice. Thoreau never ceased to elevate such experiences and to couch them in economic terms. He describes weeks when "idleness was the most attractive and productive industry. Many a forenoon I have stolen away, preferring to spend thus the most valued part of the day; for I was rich if not in money, in sunny hours and summer days, and spent them lavishly; nor do I regret that I did not waste more of them in the workshop or the teacher's desk."

Were it not for the Colorado River, I might have been a rich man by now. Thoreau had his pond, Bataille had his sacrifices, and I—thanks to a family who preferred river trips to paychecks—had desert canyons. I can't say how many hours I have wasted there, but I've been working to fill in that time sheet my whole life—evenings around blazing campfires, the river rolling by, bare feet absorbing the day's heat from the sand. And I do not regret that I did not waste more of them in front of a blinking computer screen.

Toward the end of his essay on the Colorado River Delta, Aldo Leopold offered some sound advice. "It is the part of wisdom never to revisit a wilderness," he wrote. "To return not only spoils a trip, but tarnishes a memory. It is only in the mind that shining adventure remains forever bright."

Good thinking. The wilderness that Leopold canoed through at the head of the Gulf of California is gone, converted by one hundred years of progress to what has been called a wasteland. But the dead parts of the delta—like clearcuts, tar sands pits, and nuclear blast sites—aren't wastelands so much as they are *used* lands, the by-product(ivity) of capitalism's unmitigated success. The truly wasted lands can be found in our wilderness areas, our national parks, and our protected public lands. America's best idea, as Wallace Stegner called the park system, was to let some of our country lie fallow. If we are to believe Bataille, no matter how much we hear about the economic benefits of ecosystem services or the recreation industry, the real value of wild land is in its not being put to use. I returned to the delta and found a bit more wilderness than before thanks to a collective willingness to let some water escape our many appetites.

Leopold's essay ends with some of his more frequently quoted lines: "I am glad I shall never be young without wild country to be young in. Of what avail are forty freedoms without a blank spot on the map?" The delta as Leopold knew it may be gone as are—thanks to comprehensive satellite imagery—the blank spots on the map. But for those who are inclined to seek it out, there is still plenty of wild country in the Colorado River basin to be young in. What renders Leopold's forty freedoms meaningless is not the loss of some imagined state of pure, unaltered nature. (If that were the case, we would have lost our freedom ten thousand years ago when hunters with Clovis-point spears helped drive the mammoth to extinction.) Instead, the postmodern blank spot on the map, the twenty-first-century frontier, can be found in those places and experiences that still escape the economic order: the tang of homegrown tomato fresh off the vine, the margins in a book of poetry, a path through two-billion-year-old rock at the bottom of the Grand Canyon. These are wastelands, in the positive sense, as much as they are wildernesses, the remaining altars on which we can sacrifice our precious time.

I didn't tell anyone on the delta trip that just a few months earlier I'd kissed my mom's forehead one last time as she was loaded into a funeral-home hearse. Floating on the pulse flow, we swapped river stories instead. I felt more comfortable being scraped apart by mesquite than talking about her death to my new friends. But the night after Jorge discovered the communicating rivers, I realized for the first time that my dreams had changed. Since I arrived in Mexico she'd continued to return while I slept, still smiling and silent. But now we'd both accepted she was dead, and that was no longer the most important fact. I'd be on the banks of the river and she would float by. Instead of running, I'd face her. We'd wave from a distance, each of us on our own journey.

The pulse flow ended a few weeks later. In the years since, the groundwater, replenished from the simulated flood, has transformed barren pockets of the delta into green patches once again. A small base flow was being maintained through 2018 to help establish native species that teams of ecologists have planted. Whether or not the experiment will be repeated is up to future treaty negotiations, but ecologists have been happy with the results. Almost as soon as the water arrived, birdlife flew out of La Ciénega de Santa Clara and Rio Hardy wetlands to investigate. The Nature Conservancy reported, "The abundance and diversity of birds in the floodplain of the Colorado River in Mexico increased after the 2014 pulse flow, with the highest concentrations in the restoration sites. . . . All told, nineteen species of conservation interest increased 49 percent from 2013 to 2015."

The treaty provision that made the pulse flow possible called the released water an "Intentionally Created Surplus." Which is to say that it was wasted. On purpose. For the birds, in both the literal and colloquial senses of the phrase. We dumped water on the ground and it disappeared, just as the gas station cashier had claimed. But waste, when considered from a perspective beyond narrow self-interest, has another name. It's called sharing.

Back at the start of our paddle across the delta, as we prepared to launch our boats at the culverts, a mother and daughter approached us. When I crouched down to talk to the girl, a toddler dressed only in a white shirt hanging past her knees, she ran and hid, peeking at me shyly from around the folds of her mother's dress. "She seems scared now," her mother told me in Spanish, "but you should have seen her yesterday. She ran right down and started playing in the water. Each time she splashed in it, she laughed. She started running up and down shouting, '*Agua! Agua!*' It was the first time she'd ever seen a river."

J ason Nez wears a wool vest, scuffed boots, and a look of total concentration. We're on the remote eastern rim of the Grand Canyon in the Navajo Nation where Nez has taken me to talk about archaeology. Beside a yucca, he pauses and picks up a small stone. One of its edges has been subtly sharpened into a cutting tool by a former resident of the area, perhaps one thousand years ago. Holding it between his thumb and forefinger, Nez stoops to cleanly slice off a fistful of ricegrass. "It's been a while since anybody cut with that," he says, dropping the tool where he found it.

Our destination is an undeveloped overlook above the Grand Canyon, but Nez is in no rush to get there. A few minutes later, he stops his pickup in a seldom-used campsite. Again he scours the area, squinting at the bright day from underneath his cowboy hat. I wonder if more artifacts are in store. "There." He points at shallow depressions in the hardened mud. "That's where a truck turned around. The dirt must have been a little wet." He takes a few steps and notes a cleared space where somebody set up a tent.

Though he's an archaeologist by trade, Nez isn't fixated on the distant past. The campsite and the ancient tool hold his attention equally. For Nez, there is no clean break between prehistory and modernity but a continuous human story that's been unfolding on this landscape since the first hunters followed bison herds to the rim of the Grand Canyon roughly 11,500 years ago.

61

"You used to go to the national parks and there would be signs that said, 'the mysterious Anasazi disappeared,'" Nez tells me. "We need to reeducate the world that Native people never left."

Nez, who recently turned forty, grew up bouncing between extended family members on the western part of the Navajo Nation near the Grand. Boyhood days spent rounding up lost sheep with his grandfather were his first career training. A skilled tracker, like a skilled archaeologist, reads stories told by traces on the land, Nez says. "If you let that landscape talk to you, it will. It will pull you. It will guide you. And Native people—we've been doing that for thousands of years."

Fifteen years ago, Nez landed an interpretive job at Navajo National Monument and stayed for two seasons while studying environmental science in Flagstaff. When he heard a research team was excavating a prehistoric dwelling on the reservation, Nez visited the site out of curiosity. He ended up joining the crew as an archaeological technician, screening buckets of dirt for small artifacts. He spent seven years with the Navajo Nation Archaeology Department, before he took a seasonal job in Grand Canyon National Park. More recently he has worked as a fire archaeologist for the park service, helping fire crews protect cultural resources across the western US. The jobs are sporadic and when he has off-time he returns to help his family herd livestock on the reservation near Tuba City.

Nez sees his Diné heritage as one of his most important assets as a researcher, and he tries to "blend tradition and science" in the field. Once, an intuitive hunch pulled Nez through the aftermath of a forest fire to a specific spot near the North Rim of the Grand. There, barely poking from a drift of white ash, was a Clovis spearpoint dating to the woolly mammoth hunts of the Ice Age. "The Force led me to it," he says, a mischievous smile breaking across his face. Nez tells me to turn around in the passenger seat of his truck and identify a sticker on his back window; it's the red symbol from Luke Skywalker's pilot helmet in Star Wars.

"So people know I'm part of the Rebellion," he explains.

While working in the Grand Canyon, Nez has studied every-thing from archaic hunting camps to eleventh-century pueblos tucked under sandstone alcoves. Native American clans in the area still trace their lineage to the cliff dwellings. "The Grand Canyon isn't just a canyon," he says. "It isn't just a river. It's not just Teddy Roosevelt. The canyon is people, living people, out there right now on the Navajo reservation, the Hopi reservation, the Zuni reserva-tion, the Hualapai, the Havasupai reservations."

Nez swings his pickup into another turnaround and gets out. I follow him down rock ledges for a hundred yards. All at once, the canyon opens before us. Three thousand feet below, the powder-blue streak of the travertine-rich Little Colorado River flows into the larger green Colorado.

Sitting on the rim, Nez tells me the legend of a Diné hero named the Dreamer who once lived on the San Juan River in southern Utah. The Dreamer climbed into a hollow log one day and rode down the San Juan to the Colorado River and into the Grand Canyon. Nez says the Hopi have a similar story, and he's convinced the legend was inspired by a historical person.

"So you don't think John Wesley Powell was the first one to float the canyon?" I ask.

Nez smiles again. "No way," he says.

(2018)

THE CONFLUENCE

Winter 2015

When the warning sirens scream above the adobe walls of Richard Nixon's Western White House in San Clemente, California, there will be maybe thirty minutes to spare before the tsunami, already marching green and huge across the Pacific, crests the roofs of the ocean-view apartments on Capistrano Beach—a single beautiful breaker over a billion-dollar reef of real estate. The yachts in the nearby Dana Point Harbor will rise up and surf inland, battering through the low-lying, high-rent trailer parks tucked beneath Interstate 5. Just up the hill above Vista de Agua Boulevard, where the elevation tops four hundred feet and home values refuse to fall below a cool $1.5 million, the realtor couples with gleaming teeth, the insurance men who insure insurance companies, and the silicon women with Botox-stiffened lips will stay dry enough to stammer demands into iPhones as the cell towers overload and go down. The portions of twelve-lane interstate that survive intact will soon become the world's longest parking lot while, a few miles down the coast, the backup pumps in the San Onofre Nuclear Generating Station gurgle under sea water and give up the fight. The day traders who had the foresight to purchase private evacuation services will be plucked off the hill above Vista de Agua by helicopter before the power plant's cooling systems fail and the rods melt down and a gentle radioactive rain falls across Orange County.

Nobody will return for a thousand years. Ground zero: something to orient by.

When nanobots have finally cleaned up the radioactivity, the first archaeologists to visit the hill to study human culture before the Great Warming will arrive ten miles north of ground zero and make note of the abandoned vehicles left on the Vista de Agua mound. Teams will observe that the cars still parked in the driveways or ruined garages of the five-thousand-square-foot homes on the hill are stratified according to twenty-first-century notions of wealth. The lowest levels, they'll notice, are ringed by BMW and Lexus sedans. Above are sports cars: Mercedes, Porsche, and Tesla. And on the crowning heights of the hill, in the six-car garage by the Olympic-size, kidney-shaped swimming pool, they will discover the remains of a Ferrari, a Lamborghini, and an Aston Martin.

Everything will be in its place, except this: a rusted-out Subaru parked beside a travel trailer in the shadow of yet another minor mansion (at the BMW level of the hill). Lab analysis will reveal a blanket of orange shag carpeting once swathed the interior of the trailer. The hatchback, trailer, and carpet will spawn many theories. A great unconformity of income, an anomaly in an ordered world.

This is the scenario playing out in my mind as I drive past Riverside and San Bernardino on the 15, a route that always gives me visions of the apocalypse. An hour earlier, I left my girlfriend and her Subaru back in the fallout radius of the San Onofre plant along with 8.5 million other people. She understands that such selfish measures are necessary. In a few days, she will be off on a trip to Yosemite.

We've been in California for five months. Five months that I've spent in a cubicle in front of a laptop in the folds of cyberspace where all information is equally near and far and the direct deposits arrive every two weeks—my first office job. Five months sleeping in a musty camper trailer that stays parked in the side yard of a kind software engineer who charters a sailboat every weekend and heads toward Santa Catalina Island. For me, it's been five months in exile from the redrock of the Colorado Plateau. But now I'm getting out.

The traffic is clearing. The asphalt under my wheels is beautiful. The San Andreas Fault is silent, for now. There is a whitewater kayak strapped to my roof, and I'm heading for Arizona where I've got a date with a flash flood.

Two ravens call to each other, their voices like weathered gate hinges in animated conversation. My friend Will and I are packing our kayaks in the parking lot of a gas station on the Navajo Nation along the red dust edge of canyon country. It's been twenty-four hours since I left California. We load bags into our boats, drag our kayaks across a plain of drying silt, and shoulder through a line of tamarisk to the banks of the Little Colorado River.

The water slides past in slow boils, giving off a dank, metallic smell. This land is remembering what it means to rot, what it means to rust. The mud river before us absorbs the mid-morning sun and reflects it back, not as a glittering mirror, but with the glow of a blacksmith's forge. The entire channel pulses in a dance of molten bronze.

I've been tracking this water through online hydrographs since the storm hit near the Arizona-New Mexico line fifty-four hours ago. It fell as a downpour in the lowlands and as wet snow in the ponderosa forests along the Mogollon Rim. The bed of the Little Colorado River had been dry for weeks, but as the rainwater ran through the flats, the rising sun hit the heavy snow above. Soon, a hungry wall of foam was weaving down sandy creek beds. The flood consumed dark nests of greasewood and tumbleweed until it was more flesh than liquid—a ravenous invertebrate feeding off of gravity, absorbing new tributaries, growing, sniffing out the Grand Canyon 250 miles away and thousands of feet below.

Now the rainwater has arrived in the blink-and-it's-gone town of Cameron, Arizona (my favorite kind of town), and so have we. After nine hours of driving, a rendezvous with Will in the Nevada desert, a bleary food shop at midnight in Flagstaff, and a fitful two hours of sleep, there is nothing left to do. Our drysuits are on and our lifejackets cinched. We run through final mental checklists, squeeze into our boats, and push off into the current. The last two days of frantic preparation dissipate as we slow to the river's pace. Silt sings against my boat's hull. We paddle ahead, the water and our bodies the only sources of movement on this breezeless morning. Low cliffs slope upward on either side of us as the river sinks into the canyon.

Fifty miles downstream, where the Little Colorado flows into the Colorado River proper and into Grand Canyon National Park, developers are pushing to build a multi-billion-dollar resort. The Grand Canyon Escalade tramway, as it's being called, would include boutique hotels and restaurants on the canyon rim as well as a cable gondola capable of depositing more than ten thousand people per day onto a "River Walk" development near the confluence. Tourists would be able to order corndogs and ice cream within spitting distance of the Little Colorado's terminus, a place that today is most commonly reached on a river trip of more than two hundred miles, or a tough multi-day hike.

I use the word *spitting* intentionally. For many traditional members of the tribal nations in the region, the tramway proposal is as insulting as a great gob of phlegm, drawn from deep and with plenty of noise, being flung directly at a holy sanctum. The Hopi recall that the powder-blue springs, which emerge from the bottom of the Little Colorado gorge, mark the exact place where humanity first climbed out of the earth from the wet underground Third World and entered the dry crust of the Fourth World that we still inhabit today. They insist that the spring near the confluence is ground zero of a different kind. The center. The origin.

For centuries, the confluence belonged to no one. No settlements were built on the canyon floor, and those that passed through did so as pilgrims. Warring clans would turn a blind eye to enemies on the pilgrimage route. But when the US government drew lines around the Hopi and Navajo reservations in the late 1800s, the confluence went to the Diné. And while the Little Colorado River is also sacred in Diné culture, it's not seen as the origin of humanity. Today the reservation suffers 40 percent unemployment, and the promise of jobs is compelling for some. The Diné have split over the development proposal. Meanwhile, Hopi lawyers are preparing to stop the Escalade before any survey stakes are pounded into the canyon's rim.

I'm here to see the Little Colorado for myself, to ride a flash flood to the confluence while the tram is still being debated.

I stop paddling and stare into the river. The floodwater is boiling. Sediment rises to the surface in upcurrents the size of watermelons. The center of each boil is chalky white with the finest silt and is gradated in every shade of brown-red to where it meets the dark seam of the next boil. A perfect pattern in the turmoil. I sweep my paddle across the borderlines and send all the colors swirling together, whirlpools spinning out from the center of impact. Chaos, pattern, disturbance, chaos. Eleven months ago my mom died. From before I could walk, she brought me to desert rivers. She taught me to love these silty waters. She, too, is part of why I'm here.

A black tree branch twists out of the flood like a skeletal claw scraping at the sky.

When I first learned to talk, my mom asked me if I remembered being born. "It hurt," I said without hesitation. I can't remember any longer. My earliest moments are shrouded in darkness, and so too for so many of my fellow non-native Americans. We can't turn our necks to look back for our origins. Instead, we face our future with fused vertebrae, always staring ahead. We gaze past the sprawling cities and thickening atmosphere and see the fulfillment of our quest for wealth and ease. White developers peer down from the cliffs of the Navajo Nation and into the Grand Canyon. They imagine people lining up to swipe credit cards. They tell Diné communities, This little tram will be a ticket out for your suffering people. We'll team up. We'll provide the capital, you provide the land, and the jobs will spread. Some Diné people say they've heard this before, when the white people wanted the land for coal or when they discovered uranium. Now the developers have found a loophole to bring tourists into Grand Canyon National Park without having to deal with park restrictions on development. They will use Navajo land. The bargain is the same, the new resource is tourism, but the jobs are just as needed as ever.

Will the tourists come? Of course they will. Everyone wants to stand at the bottom of the Grand Canyon as easily as on its rim. Why walk when you can be carried? In America, we tell ourselves that there is value in hard work, but only in work that ends in getting paid. And we're paid so we can buy freedom from exertion. So we can relax.

"This is the desert," writes poet Richard Shelton. "It is all we have left to destroy."

Will pulls over beneath a large sandstone boulder on the shore and climbs up its most lenient facet with his camera. A photographer and filmmaker, Will is always searching for the right place to "get the shot." He finds the vantage point he's looking for and asks me to take several laps in the eddy beneath him.

I know the drill. A few years ago, Will and I spent six months together on the river while we paddled 1,700 miles from the source of the Green River in Wyoming to its confluence with the Colorado River in Utah and on to the Gulf of California in Mexico. We returned to the source of the Colorado River in Rocky Mountain National Park the following summer and paddled down to Nevada again. Will's camera was always handy, and all too often I was the most convenient human subject. For the last few years, we've drifted our separate ways, Will moving to Washington State while I eddied out in California. But when I sent out an email to kayaker friends a few weeks earlier to say I was keeping an eye on flash floods in northern Arizona, I knew Will would be the most likely to drop everything at twenty-four hours' notice and join me.

When Will gives a thumbs-up from behind his viewfinder, I float to the top of the slack water, place the bow of my boat in the current, and peel out. It feels as if the front half of my kayak is barely touching the river. The stern is packed full of drybags and plastic bottles: camping gear, eighteen hard-boiled eggs, last-minute gas station snacks, and, since the river water is far too silty to be filtered or boiled, four gallons of water. It's all we have to get us fifty-five miles downstream to the Colorado River and to sustain us through a three-mile, three-thousand-vertical-foot climb out of the canyon. This has to be the heaviest boat I've ever paddled.

Before Will has sealed his camera in his drybag and climbed down from the boulder, I'm paddling downstream, trying to make up for our late start and immediate photographic delay. We could run out of water in two ways: Our four gallons of drinking water could be too little, or the rain-fueled river could dry up beneath our kayaks, leaving us knee-deep in mud at the bottom of the Grand Canyon. Or both.

We cruise beneath the gray limbs of cottonwoods, leafless with winter. The canyon walls stretch higher and close in on the river. "It looks like we're going into a mini Marble Canyon," Will remarks as the river carves through the same constricting layers of rock we've passed before in the first hours of the two Grand Canyon trips we've taken together—cliffs of Kaibab Limestone, crumbling slopes of the Toroweap Formation. On his 1869 exploration of the Colorado River, John Wesley Powell named the sixty-one-mile stretch below Lee's Ferry "Marble Canyon." Though it contains no marble, in places its limestone cliffs resemble marble stained red by iron in the layers above. What was then known as the Big Canyon technically begins at the confluence of the Little Colorado and Colorado Rivers. Powell would promote the adjective from *big* to *grand* several years later.

This canyon is similar to Marble Canyon but more intimate; its walls press in tighter, its entrenched meanders are more exaggerated. When we enter the harder Coconino Sandstone, the canyon squeezes to a twisting channel just twenty feet across, the river touching the cliffs on either side. We stop for more photos beneath an old sheep bridge that crosses the narrows.

In 1902, John Muir wrote, "Nature has a few places beyond man's power to spoil—the ocean, the two icy ends of the globe, and the Grand Canyon." We've been busy challenging this statement in the century since. Plastic may soon outweigh fish in the oceans, and the ends of the globe are far less icy than they were in Muir's time. The Grand Canyon, for its part, has become the second-most-visited national park in the country, its edges dotted with uranium mines, and its ends sealed off by the two largest reservoirs in the US. Though few would call the Grand spoiled today, even fewer would still think of it as unspoilable. The Sierra Club, which Muir would go on to found, led the fight to stop dam builders from turning the length of the canyon into a series of reservoirs in the 1950s and '60s, and that conservation legacy has survived. Rafters who traverse the Grand Canyon's 277-mile length from Lee's Ferry to the Grand Wash Cliffs pass one highway bridge four miles from the boat ramp, a pair of footbridges at Phantom Ranch, and a dirt takeout at Diamond Creek. Only a handful of manmade structures are visible on the rim over the course of the trip, and a strict permit system limits the number of rafting parties in the canyon at any given time. For hikers willing to break away from the main thoroughfares of the Bright Angel and Kaibab Trails, the canyon is a maze of pathways through side canyons, scree slopes, and dead ends where few venture.

Edward Abbey said we should preserve the Grand Canyon because it may one day serve as a guerilla stronghold against a tyrannical government. Perhaps. But we also need it right now. We need the canyon because it resists the flattening and compression of landscape. Today, you can drive out to the nearest interstate and cross from one end of the country to the other following the same green exit signs. You can sleep in the same hotels and eat in the same restaurants. You can open your phone and see the same websites regardless of your location. Unique, grounded spaces are facing an extinction crisis along with so many species. But wild places, where phone signals fail and the reach of corporate familiarity ends, provide anchors against the disorienting effects of a uniform globalized culture. When you walk or paddle through a landscape, no two places are alike.

In 1768, a world away from the desert, Immanuel Kant noticed that this trend was underway. He'd never left the eastern Prussian town he was born in, and he never would. But nonetheless he felt the Enlightenment fixation on reason—which he was helping to usher in—had stripped the world of orienting cultural and ethical landmarks. Space, Kant contended, could be thought of as an endless three-dimensional grid, but without a centerpoint there was no hope of finding one's bearing. As religion loosened its grip on Europe, there was no longer a Jerusalem or a Mecca to turn to; people drifted through Prussia according to the fickle tides of business. So Kant came up with a good Enlightenment answer to this problem. The individual, he said, is the center. The ego serves as the origin point where the x, y, and z axes meet. And from that center, a cogent world can unfold. Wherever you go, there you are—right in the middle of things.

In his book *God is Red*, Standing Rock Sioux scholar Vine Deloria Jr. sees this Kantian view of space as symptomatic of a cultural malaise. He makes the case that Western culture in general, and Christianity in particular, has always been more concerned with the individual and the temporal than with the spatial and the communal. Even today, the Christian prophecy of the Second Coming has been secularized into our fixation with technological progress—which we're told will one day deliver us to an earthly paradise. Tribal cultures, by contrast, are tied to a specific landscape. "The vast majority of Indian tribal religions," Deloria writes, "have a sacred center at a particular place, be it a river, a mountain, a plateau, valley, or other natural feature." The center was a common reference point for a community of people in the context of a more-than-human world. Sacred places, Deloria says, "properly inform us that we are not larger than nature and that we have responsibilities to the rest of the natural world that transcend our own personal desires and wishes." From the orienting center of a sacred place emerges an ethics embedded in the physical and the shared.

In some cases, climbing to the top of the sacred mountain was forbidden. In others, sacred places could be visited with proper spiritual and ceremonial preparation. But regardless, these places almost always required a physically demanding journey beyond the confines of the village or hunting grounds to reach. Even the Latin word *sacrare*, from which the English "sacred" is derived, means "to set apart."

In the city we all tend to become Kantians, the centers of our own private universes. But according to Deloria, to live with no external reference point is to be unhinged, narcissistic, delusional—the sicknesses of Europe. To become oriented, according to many traditions, we have to journey away from the familiar and into the unknown. The world is not coherent simply by using ourselves as the primary reference point; it is through the walkabout, the pilgrimage, the quest, that we begin to understand our place in the greater community.

Floating down the Little Colorado, it feels as if we've rediscovered a lost corner of the Colorado Plateau. With each turn of the canyon, we're etching lines on a map and placing ourselves within it. Not many people pass through this corridor in a given year. When the river isn't flowing, few backpackers attempt to hike from Cameron to the confluence—clay and quicksand, or a complete lack of drinking water, make the fifty-five-mile trek brutal for foot travel. Paddling is faster, but Will and I have yet to hear of any paddler who's ridden a flood to the confluence more than once, owing to intermittent flows and the three-mile-long climb at the takeout. When we pull over for lunch, we see no footprints on the ground. No fire rings. No signs of campers. While local tribes tell tales of great events in this area, it's all too easy for me to see it as empty—uninhabited and uninhabitable. *It's like having your own private Grand Canyon*, I keep thinking as the walls continue to grow above us, in places stretching from river to rim in a thousand sheer feet.

We do, however, see plenty of trash riding downstream with us—drink bottles, oil jugs, and basketballs—a mind-boggling number of basketballs circulating in eddies or caught in strainers. Like us, the debris has been waiting for the flood. I imagine the balls escaping schoolyard courts on the Hopi reservation or bouncing away from hard dirt driveways in Winslow. They've rolled off mesa tops and settled into arroyo bottoms for months or years awaiting a cloudburst. And now they're in motion again. Out of the water I pluck one that's been sanded down to a sphere of loose, gray strings.

A faded and partly deflated ball floated past as we launched, a Wilson, and we find it a useful companion. The rain upstream stopped two days ago. The faucet is off and we have to keep pace with the flood if we want to float all the way to our exit point before the river dries up. Wilson roughly marks the speed of the current. We paddle past him in slack water and watch him bob by when we stop for breaks. The three of us are keeping up a good pace despite a late start and short winter days. Will and I finish the afternoon with an hour-long sprint, leaving Wilson to passively navigate the eddy lines. By the time we make camp on a small beach that evening, we've covered twenty-three miles.

While Will starts dinner, I climb the steep drainage above camp to look for water. Ledges of Redwall Limestone are worn smooth in the lowest part of the channel, and I'm confident I'll be able to find some deep pocket holding rain from the last storm. We've only had a few sips of water all day, but dinner and breakfast tomorrow will start to drain our jugs. If we can refill them even once, the pressure of getting into and out of the canyon on our four plastic gallons will be greatly relieved.

The first shelf yields nothing, just a polished slope of gray rock. The second dips back on itself, but the pool is filled only with wet gravel. The rains did fall here briefly, at least. I climb higher until I'm straining to see our camp in the settling dusk. Above I find a tiny depression holding about a quart of cool water. Palms to the rock, I lower my lips to the pool and drink deeply until plumes of fine silt rise to the surface like smoke. I pick my way back down the cliffs by headlamp.

Will has built a small campfire in an aluminum foil pan to catch the ashes. Sitting in its glow, we talk about something other than logistics. A few years ago, we were college roommates, and we run through a list of our friends: who is still dirtbagging between climbing routes or rivers or ski areas in the back of their van, who has fallen into careers or grad school. Will outlasted me, somehow, in this game of middle-class chicken. In college, I made bold proclamations against income while throwing around phrases like "voluntary simplicity." I got rid of my cell phone during junior year to save the thirty-dollar–per-month bill. I took calls on the landline in my apartment room (free) and made outgoing calls on my cheap laptop (also free). I would spend twenty dollars per week on food: oatmeal for breakfast and a giant pot of vegetable and bean slop made every Sunday to sustain me through the week of philosophy classes. (I ignored Thoreau's dictum, cribbed from Pythagoras, that flatulence makes philosophical meditations impossible.) Will joined my food program for a while until he wanted to spend too much money on organic fruits and we had to start cooking separately. I had standards. But now I'm the one who moved to SoCal for a salaried editing job at a magazine, while Will has been making films in Tibet about rivers that are about to be dammed to power the booming Chinese economy. I may be living in a trailer, but Will is still living out of his drybag.

He needles me about my career.

"The best part of selling out is getting paid," I tell him.

Will picked up a parasitic yeast somewhere in his travels and, at the advice of an acupuncturist, has cut back on carbs. For dinner, we eat lentils. "Slop," says Will, "just like the old days." He pulls out two gas station cigars and hands one to me.

I wake as the stars are beginning to fade. I unrolled my sleeping bag below the low limbs of a juniper to prevent the frost from settling on it, and I lay there for a while trying to keep track of the disappearing constellations. When there's enough light to move about, I rise and snap twigs into a homemade wood cookstove fashioned from a tin can to boil water for coffee. Will wakes. He pulls on a light down coat and kneels beside the pot, his hands held out to the tiny blaze. Will brings out a dozen hard-boiled eggs in their cardboard case. We crack open three eggs apiece and season them with a bottle of habanero salsa.

As we pack our camping gear into small drybags and shove them into the sterns of our boats, I supplement the breakfast with a quarter bagel slathered with peanut butter: fuel for the cold miles ahead. We put on fleece layers, thawed from the night's brief freeze but still damp from yesterday, and step into our drysuits.

The first Class IV rapid appears before noon. From the eddy above I can see distinct spouts of water exploding skyward—a hole. Normally a feature like that would churn the river a frothy white, but this is no normal river. Jets shoot from the hole in sluggish, opaque ropes, casting shadows behind them in the sunlight. This mesmerizing liquid can hardly be called water. It's so muddy, so viscous that it behaves like no water I've ever seen. Like some shimmerless relative of mercury, it's impossible to see a millimeter below the river's surface, and, like mercury, it clings thickly to itself even as it breaks apart in the rapid.

I turn out of the eddy and paddle left across the current, aiming for a narrow channel below the hole where most of the river is being squeezed between a cliff face and a school-bus-sized boulder. To the right of the slot, the river disappears into a jumble of broken rocks—a sieve, one of whitewater's most dangerous features. Enough flow is heading to the right that a kayak could be sucked into the rock pile and not make it out the other side. I avoid the hole and straighten into the wave train to line up with the slot. Right on target until a solid *smack* lands on my boat's hull. It spins me backwards and to the right. It's as if one of those spring-loaded boxing gloves from cartoons had been triggered right below my kayak, knocking me toward the sieve. With my bow pointing upstream, I angle to the cliff face. I dig my paddle in against the current to slow my descent into the rock pile fifteen feet below. Frantic upstream strokes move me slowly toward the main channel, but they're not enough to counter the pull of the sieve. *Got . . . to . . . make . . . it.* I spin perpendicular to the current and land a few more strokes. It's just enough to put me in front of the school bus boulder, a pillow of water billowing off its face in a kind of wave. I allow my boat to catch in the pillow sideways and surf toward the slot. Just before I'm pulled through, I glance back at the deadly rock pile. A cracked, orange basketball is rolling in place as the river is siphoned straight down beneath it. *Same deflated dent. Same color. Can't be.* I see the letters W-I-L . . . and I'm whisked through the slot to safety.

Downstream, the rapids continue to play tricks. The visual cues I'm accustomed to subconsciously processing when running rapids—signs that indicate hidden rock or standing wave—are confused here. Other chunks of limestone lay invisible just beneath the surface waiting to knock me off line. Pour-overs churn in dark pockets, appearing only when I'm on top of them. A single splash to the face leaves a fine film of earth in my eyes so that everything seems veiled in a brownish-red fog—the color of the river, the color of the canyon. Will's face is painted with dirt, which pulls and cracks when he speaks.

This is no river, this is a flood. I've seen storms hit canyon country before, dozens of waterfalls streaming off sandstone cliffs in southern Utah or jets exploding from notches in black schist on the Colorado River. I once walked beside potholes strung along the floor of a fossil-rich limestone canyon. The day was over one hundred degrees with only a few clouds in the sky, and I startled tadpoles each time I stopped to drip the clear water on my neck. A crack of thunder, and twenty minutes later I was scrambling for high ground as frothing brown waterfalls connected the pools with tadpoles in tow.

As a kayaker, witnessing the formation of an instant river in the desert is painfully enticing. It's as if a Midwestern rock climber were able to watch, in a matter of minutes, an unclimbed face of Yosemite granite rise out of Nebraska's cornfields. The question is always the same: Could I paddle it and survive? Nearly every time the answer is no—slot canyons and ephemeral waterfalls don't make for the cleanest rapids. Here on the Little Colorado, however, I'm riding a rainstorm. There's an elegance in that fact. To meet the rain pulse, we had to plan, prepare, track water across hundreds of miles, and get to the put-in on time. A flash flood is a concentration of weather and landscape moving to its own wild whims, forces beyond our little Kantian egos.

Pausing for a lunch of nuts and meat sticks, Will jumps into one of his lectures. As an environmental science major, but also a student of Zen, he enjoys analyzing the world through theories that border on the preposterous. "My drysuit was starting to wear out and seep water after I got some punctures on my last trip to China, but I think the LCR fixed it," he says, using our shorthand for the Little Colorado River. "Now all the holes are clogged up with dirt." He tries to keep a straight face. "Maybe we could sell bottles of this stuff. 'Bring old Gore-Tex back to life with the restorative powers of the LCR!'" He breaks into a rapid-fire voice to list the side effects. "Potentially fatal if consumed. May cause temporary blindness. Not available in all areas. Definitely causes staining."

The rapids come in quick succession all afternoon, though none require advance scouting. We paddle under a wall that rises two thousand feet straight up from the river, painted with blacks, golds, and tans. Darkness is falling by the time we collapse on a brushy sandbar, but we've made another twenty-five miles. That only leaves us two miles to the Hopi Salt Trail: our exit point. The trail is the last feasible place where we'll be able to hike our kayaks back to the rim without making an illegal descent of the permitted Colorado River, but it means we'll have to stash our boats six miles above the confluence and hike to the proposed tram site. Two miles of paddling plus twelve miles of hiking round trip. No problem.

A line is being drawn at the confluence eight miles below our campsite. I can picture it from my sleeping bag. Though the Little Colorado carries only an eighth of the flow of the Colorado, it's supplying all of the sediment. The larger river is cold and clear from its sojourn five hundred feet under Lake Powell.

As the Colorado descends into the cataracts of the Marble Canyon above the confluence, it forms waves that can fling passengers from a loaded eighteen-foot raft like a horse shooing away a fly with the flick of its tail. But at the same time, it feels somehow bloodless. Emptied of sediment and chilled to an unnatural forty-two degrees by the Glen Canyon Dam, the river has made a thousand-mile journey to get to the Grand Canyon. It has learned what it means to be manipulated. It has toured homes and wastewater treatment plants. It has been held behind reservoirs and pushed through turbines. It has been broken off into ditches and soaked through alfalfa fields. It has seen large parts of its flow taken across mountain ranges or injected in natural gas wells two miles below the river.

The flooding Little Colorado, by contrast, has known no resistance. Three days ago, it began to form as rain peeled dirt off the bedrock in sheets. Boulders dislodged and shifted. Grains of sand, cemented in sandstone waves for hundreds of millions of years, were pulled loose. Even riverbanks failed to contain the flood as it drove around corners, spilling out into sagebrush and down waterfalls. All that time it was building power. Now, as it courses down into the Grand Canyon, its headwaters have ceased to run. The snows have either melted off or settled into tree wells to wait for spring. High in the basin, the river has turned to stream, then trickle, then chain of stagnant pools surrounded by mud flats, acres of breaking polygons already peeling up at the edges.

Naturalist Ann Zwinger reports that in a single storm, the Little Colorado can flush the equivalent of nine inches of topsoil per square mile downstream. Even before the dams, when the Colorado ran unfettered, the Little Colorado still had the power to impress by contrast. In 1869, the Powell expedition camped at the confluence. One of the boatmen, George Bradley, wrote the Little Colorado was "a lothesome [sic] little stream, so filthy and muddy that it fairly stinks." Jack Sumner, another expedition member, concurred, calling the confluence "a miserable lonely place indeed, with no signs of life but lizards, bats and scorpions. It seemed like the first gates of hell."

Will and I haven't paddled five minutes the next morning when our loathsome little stream disappears. A perfect horizon line crosses in front of us and a low roar is all the indication we have of what's below. The river is fanning out into the tamarisk and we have to wade and bushwhack our way to get to solid ground. We've entered the travertine zone of the canyon and found the run's hardest rapid: Atomizer. The eight-mile stretch between Atomizer and the confluence is the only section of the Little Colorado that has water year-round, thanks to a number of springs. The spring water—rich in chloride, sodium, calcium, and bicarbonate—leaves dam-like deposits of minerals across the river that create a unique type of rapid. At Atomizer, the river plunges over tiered falls with no single channel down the center. Paddling down it is a matter of scraping your way off the drops, trying not to get caught in the holes that lurk below, and avoiding at all costs the travertine caves on both sides that could swallow a boat or body whole. I take one look and decide to walk. Will has been paddling Class V rapids several times a week while living in the whitewater hub of White Salmon, Washington. He styles the line, plopping over each terrace without losing momentum and expertly dodging the caves.

Downstream, half a dozen more horizon lines are stacked in a two-mile-long staircase. The rapids are easier, but the scouting is time-consuming. We hack through brush, climb up sharp travertine boulders, and plot our course through the drops. All of this slows our progress.

By the time we unpack our gear at the foot of the steep side canyon where the Hopi Salt Trail climbs to the rim, it's well past noon. People have used this trail for thousands of years to descend from mesa-top communities into the Little Colorado and a sacred salt seep just downstream from the confluence. While the seep's minerals are no longer needed for physiological survival, it, along with the springs, maintains an immense significance for Navajo, Hopi, Zuni, and other tribes. And between the trail and the seep, a few miles from us, lies the blue spring where the Hopi say humankind first emerged.

We change, eat, and begin half-jogging down the lower part of the trail in an effort to pull off the twelve-mile round-trip hike to the confluence before dark. Getting to the Colorado means completing our mission: standing on the base of the proposed tram site where tourists may one day snap photos behind railings on the canyon floor. It also means clear water. At the confluence, we will be able to fill enough jugs to get us up the Salt Trail and back to the road.

That plan doesn't last long. With the river high, the trail is mostly flooded out and we're forced to dodge around, or crawl through, thicket after thicket of skin-tearing mesquite. We cut to the boulder fields along the cliff edge and back again to the riverside reeds in a zigzag of frustration. I keep thinking a path will appear around the next bend or the next, even as the light starts to soften on the cliffs.

Will calls from fifty feet behind me. I can't see him, but I can tell where he is from the rustling of a willow patch. I wait until he emerges. "We should turn around," he says. "We're less than a third of the way there, and even if we stop now it'll still be dark by the time we get back."

I think about the shrinking gallon of water we still have between us and the river downstream. "Let me try to get a view from the top of those boulders," I say, pointing ahead. "If there's still no trail, we'll figure out our plan B."

Will agrees. I head toward the high point but something shiny stops me in my tracks. I bend down and pull the foil remnants of a freeze-dried backpacking dinner from the dirt. Beside it is a shredded Ziploc. And a pair of shorts. I scan the rest of the small clearing. Just ahead the padded, black waistband of a backpack is sticking from the sand.

"Will!" I shout. "Come check this out."

We pull the backpack out of the dirt and flip it with a stick. More meal packets and crusted clothes tumble out. A decaying raincoat and sports bra are buried underneath, packed with sediment. It's clear the owner has long since departed, but I can't tell whether the backpack has sat here for six months or several years. Will scatters its contents, looking for an ID, something bearing a name or a phone number. Explanations race through my mind. Maybe the backpacker left her overnight gear and set out for a day hike. There could have been a flash flood in a slotted side canyon, or a fall. Maybe, like us, she was unable to find any rain-storing potholes and couldn't get to the Colorado to refill. Did she resort to drinking from the turquoise waters of the lower Little Colorado only to vomit up what little liquid was left in her stomach? Maybe there was a rescue. And maybe there wasn't. The discovery crumples our whole agitated quest for the confluence back into the present moment. Our descent down this trackless canyon, with its star-strewn nights and raging flood, has only whispered what the backpack now says clearly: you are out there.

I squat in the dirt before the decaying artifacts. The backpack is sobering, like nearly losing your balance at the top of a cliff. On a map, we're technically in the Little Colorado River Navajo Tribal Park just outside Grand Canyon National Park, but *park* is entirely the wrong word. It suggests the greenery and paved paths in the suburbs or the controlled thrills of a Six Flags, somewhere that might have a roller coaster—or a tram. Whoever left this camp learned that difference.

We turn back upstream. This is as close to the confluence as we'll get, but maybe the abandoned camp has been our destination all along. I thought I came here to stand at the tram site, but now I realize my real purpose is to feel the contours of a canyon while contours still matter. We're a mile into the earth. We've survived the rapids and the river. But now we have to get out—and the only way to do that is to walk.

The silty river is useless. The salty, mineral-laden spring at the foot of the Hopi Salt Trail is useless. There's water all around us, and it's all undrinkable. Running through our options, we make a plan on the hike back to camp. Tonight, we decide, we'll follow the wash up into the side canyon, looking for the elusive pothole. And if we don't find one? The question hangs in the air as we make the rest of the trek in silence.

Back at our kayaks, we poke around with our headlamps. We were in such a rush to get to the confluence when we arrived that we barely took stock of our surroundings. Near the flat patch of lightly colored gravel where we dropped our gear is what looks like a helicopter-landing pad. A tunnel has been sawed through the large mesquite trees leading back to the river, and we follow it to a clearing where planks of wood form benches between rocks. A built-up fire pit sits in the center of the campsite. Tarps are lashed over stacks of gear along its edges.

"Hello," I call out into the night, though it looks like the camp has been closed up for winter.

Will peeks under the tarps. "This is US Fish and Wildlife stuff," he says. "There's a stencil on these boxes."

The spring water that flows down the lower section of the Little Colorado is one of the last holdouts for the endangered humpback chub, which dominated the Colorado basin before the introduction of sport fish and dams. Unlike trout, which have a lower tolerance of salinity, chub are able to spawn in the Little Colorado.

A pot that's been left out on a grate over the fire ring catches my eye. I walk over and see it's an old pressure cooker with copper tubing fastened to the steam vent on its lid. The pipe rises to a five-gallon plastic bucket where it coils around and exits through the bottom. *A still* is my first thought. *Those fisheries scientists are down here making moonshine in a government camp.* But I quickly come to a more plausible explanation: we're not the first people to be caught here surrounded by undrinkable water. "A water distilling setup," I say as Will approaches.

At this point, making use of the researchers' gear sounds easier than setting off into the canyon on a blind chase for a pothole. Will goes to fill a jug with the clear, salty spring water behind our camp. I dip a bucket in the river and build a fire of mesquite branches. The inside of the pressure cooker is thick with mineral deposits like what you'd find on the edges of a hot spring, but the valve on the lid looks unclogged. Will returns and pours the spring water into the pot. We stoke the fire and position an empty bottle beneath the spout on the bucket. Soon the pot begins to rattle and shake. From the far end of the tubing, a single drop of water plunks into the waiting bottle. More twigs are added to the fire, and the drips increase in frequency to one every two seconds. In five minutes, the bottom of the bottle is almost covered. I take a sip of the condensed steam. It's lukewarm, soft, and slightly metallic, but drinkable. All salt has been left behind in the pot.

Inefficient as it is, the distilling process requires constant attention—fetch water, fill the pot, build up the fire, refill the warm water in the bucket with cool river water to speed condensation, find more firewood, and try not to check what little progress has been made in the filling bottle. "If this went any slower, you could probably keep it running twenty-four hours a day and still die of thirst," Will says.

While we're coaxing the steam along, we plan the hike ahead. The trail climbs three thousand feet over three miles. Though I'd like to start the hike with as much water as possible, we decide we can go for it when we have one gallon each. It's midnight by the time we reach that goal.

"Tomorrow will be hard," Will admits as we unpack our sleeping bags in the moonlight, "but it shouldn't take more than six hours to get to the rim." That sounds like a reasonable pace to me, and we decide not to set an alarm. For the third time in twenty-four hours we've vastly overestimated our own abilities.

That night, I dream I'm floating weightless underwater. Light hangs in green webs. There's a bright center to the light with blackness all around, and I calmly breaststroke toward it. My throat itches to breathe, but sunlight has begun to outweigh darkness. The surface is near when a current pulls from my right side, a whirlpool yanking me down. I realize I'm in a reservoir, caught in the drag of the turbine intake. I kick harder. My lungs burn.

I've heard it said that the easiest way to die in the desert is either thirst or drowning. But now I know: drowning *is* an infinite thirst. Not a Sahara dehydration—tongue like rough sandstone, head pounding, feet stumbling toward an imagined oasis, skin cracking with the hallucinating mind. Not that. A thirst more urgent. First, the lungs expand and contract behind a closed mouth while the swimmer's strokes flail. A point of heat starts in the chest and radiates outward until every cell is screaming in dry fire, made more insane by the proximity of the solution: cool water pressing into nostrils, along the seam of the lips. To drink is to quench that thirst. The turbines are near. Heat, heat, heat. I draw in a breath and out go the flames.

Under cold moonlit canyon walls, I wake coughing.

It's fully light by the time we finish the last of our eggs and cram gear into boats. We've brought along backpack straps that attach to the kayaks. We tighten them down, readjust their lengths, and shift heavier gear from bow to stern. The climb begins, the noses of our eight-foot-long boats dragging on the uneven path behind us. When a bump sends the whole load swaying, we have to stop with a wide stance so as not to topple over.

The trail switchbacks up as erratically as a bent paperclip. The sun's heat reflects off the rocks. Ten minutes in, a water bottle escapes from Will's kayak and we watch it bounce downhill. It's nearly back in our camp by the time it stops. He lowers his boat and hikes down. Fifty yards later, the trail dips off a small cliff and we have to lower the boats by hand. The backpack straps are useful only so long as we're carrying the boats. Should we slip, the system threatens to pull us back down the hill, body locked to a bouncing, 115-pound version of Will's water bottle. More upclimbs and low overhangs follow, where the boats must be set down and dragged. Hours pass. The rim towers thousands of feet above us.

Once, in a moment of youthful indiscretion, I went to a gym. I was a freshman in college, living in a city for the first time in my life, and I thought that's what adults in cities did. I got on the StairMaster, put it on the hard setting, and plugged into a rerun of *Seinfeld*. I worked out for ten full minutes before swearing off indoor exercise for good. Climbing out of the Grand Canyon is like being on one of those machines. The difference is, each step is larger, and instead of flat plastic pedals, you're walking up loose scree and crumbling limestone ledges covered in round pieces of gravel. That, and you're balancing 115 pounds of kayak on one shoulder at the top of a cliff. Without *Seinfeld*.

A few more unnerving slips on the trail and we are forced to rethink our strategy. We unpack our boats and haul them a quarter-mile ahead, then return for our gear. The climbing is easier this way (and far less dangerous), but the distance triples: nine miles, six thousand feet up, three thousand feet down. Three quarts of water.

"I wish there was a tram in here," I say to Will, as I pass my kayak up a shelf of Redwall Limestone. This is how we sometimes talk in the backcountry. I wish I were floating in the pool at Las Vegas' Bellagio, sipping a mai tai, whatever that is. I wish someone would airdrop in a pint of Cherry Garcia. I wish there were a drinking fountain.

Freud thought jokes give expression to a repressed desire or fear that we can't bear to make fully conscious. There's plenty to want to repress: It's hot. My feet are swollen from six hours of hiking. Both shoulders are rubbed raw from carrying my kayak. We leapfrog our boats forward, try to forget our blisters, and make wishes. What are we ignoring? The jabs of pain? The possibility that we won't make it out, that our kayaks will meet the same fate as the abandoned backpack? Those are the obvious fears, too real to need repression. Maybe even more terrifying than a mid-hike injury or mind-splitting dehydration is the notion that one day this trail will no longer be a viable takeout to the Little Colorado. Who would subject themselves to the Hopi Salt Trail if there were a tram at the confluence, maybe with kayak racks on the outside of each cart? A tram would make this trip much easier, a paddle in the park. It would also make our journey an anachronism, only available to the indelibly stubborn wishing to make some kind of statement.

We're late for our planned two o'clock rendezvous with our shuttle driver, Brady, and we're still nowhere close to the road. We decide to stash our boats and make a single trip with our bags of gear. That way we have a chance of getting out before Brady calls in search and rescue at dark as we'd agreed before we left. With our drybags slung to the kayak carrying straps, we slog on.

"I wish there were an elevator here," says Will.

This is a place where distance twists. At four p.m., the trail we'd been following disappears into a near-vertical boulder field under a towering wall of sandstone. We swallow the last of our water and check our GPS. It tells us we're 2,500 feet—less than half a mile—from the trailhead. Half a mile, but a tortuous, inverted half-mile of ledges, boulders, cliffs, and rust-stained layers of millennia. Half a mile as the raven flies, but a half-mile so riddled with downdrafts and vertical gain that it seems it would be a daunting ascent even for the winged. Looking at the GPS, we crack up with laughter.

We stumble onto the two-track road at dusk just as Brady comes ripping around the corner in his truck. He hands us a jug of water and two chimichangas from the reservation gas station and tells us he's been driving the web of unmarked roads since noon. "Sure is a bitch to get here," he says. Wolfing down the greasy goodness, I nod agreement, though the ordeal is not over yet.

At three a.m., we mix instant coffee with cold water and hike back into the canyon under a nearly full moon. We use headlamps only when we have to downclimb or when the trail disappears into the rocks. By five a.m., we've reached our boats. Empty except for a bottle of water and lifejackets, the boats sit more passively in the backpack straps, less insistent about being on the ground. We make the ascent once again and crest the rim with the rising sun.

Two months later, I'm back at the Grand Canyon. I've left my California cubicle for good and followed my girlfriend to a tiny town on the edge of the Navajo Nation. I hike back down the Hopi Salt Trail, alone this time, with a rolled-up packraft, paddling gear, and an extra ration of water. The descent only takes a few hours. I inflate my packraft near the Fish and Wildlife camp with its blackened pressure cooker and launch back onto the river. Another, smaller storm awakened the Little Colorado a few days ago, once again turning the river to a brown soup.

With half an hour of easy floating, I round the bend where Will and I found the backpack after hours of bushwhacking. I paddle past the bubbling Hopi spring. Though the river isn't running its iconic milky blue color, the sheer-walled sanctuary still seems a fitting setting for the birthplace of a people. Out of respect, I do not stop. The canyon opens. I float out along the boisterous, muddy line the Little Colorado is cutting into the Colorado River and see the gates of what Powell—who stopped here for three days in 1869 to boil his rancid bacon and sift molding flour through mosquito netting—dubbed the start of Grand Canyon proper.

Tomorrow a friend's rafting trip will pick me up and carry me downstream to another trail, but for now all I have to do is wait. I sit for hours. The only sounds are the gurgles of the river, the occasional caw of a raven. As I look up to where the tram would cross the cliffs from the rim, I think back on my whole journey to this point, the trip into and out of and back into the canyon. The Colorado moves by with its steady pulse, begging to be followed.

Could I have skipped the flash flood in the first place and hiked and packrafted directly to this beach? Yes, but getting here wouldn't be as sweet now. A tourist is to a place as a person is to someone they've just met—they're strangers. I'm still a tourist, and the LCR is still mostly strange to me, but less so now that I've spent days getting to know it. That's what will be lost if the development is built: the chance for intimacy. To think entering the canyon by tram will reveal its secrets is as foolish as thinking that one can learn the mysteries of someone's heart by attending their triple bypass surgery. But I've spent days on the LCR, and the confluence is now a meaningful coordinate in my personal topography, a new ground zero.

I rise from my seat in the sand and open my drybag. Inside, I find a thin disc of oak that a friend cut for my mom's funeral service one year ago. It's only a few millimeters thick and both sides are sliced smooth through the rings of seasons. He cut hundreds of them for the crowd that gathered in a Colorado barn to see my mom off. There were slideshows and music, speeches and sobs, and we filed outside to a bridge across the Crystal River, a high tributary of the Colorado. Picking discs of oak from baskets, we scratched notes on them in pencil—notes to Ruth—before we dropped them in the river. Hundreds of messages floated downstream.

At the confluence, I give my mom an update. I write about the flood, the hike out, the hike back in, and the tram. I tell her that sacred, in the echoes of our language, means to be set apart. I walk to the bank beside where the Little Colorado joins the larger river, holding the disc in my hand. I'm about to drop it in the current, but I pause. My mom has been here before. When she married my dad, their honeymoon was a float down the Grand Canyon together. And thirty years later—two months before she was diagnosed and six months before she died—she stood right in this very spot, again in the middle of a three-week rafting trip. There's a picture of her at the confluence, laughing and healthy, unaware of the cancer in her lungs.

I never floated the Grand with my mom. I was supposed to go on that last trip, but just before it began, I was offered a job to make a film about wildlife and conservation work in the Rocky Mountains. I was fresh out of college and I wanted nothing more than to tell stories about wild places. I took the job. There would be more time, I thought, another trip, another chance. My mom understood. She never tried to talk me back into the rafting trip.

I add a line to the scribbles on the piece of oak: "I'm sorry." And I toss it in the river.

Maybe this is, in some sense, my other chance, or a chance. I beat the tram to the confluence. The point was never just to stand here, though. This place would be nothing without the context of the journey. As Townes Van Zandt sings, "Where you been is good and gone, all you keep is the getting there."

I return to my bag and write another note in my journal pages, this one to myself. I write in assertions, a proclamation, a credo, a set of directions leading back to the place where two rivers meet on the canyon floor.

In a world where distances have been shrinking for centuries, where interstates and airplanes allow us to cross thousands of miles in smooth similarity, where an internet's worth of information is always only one click away, space has been steadily losing its command over the present, almost to the point of becoming irrelevant. The Grand Canyon is a stronghold against this flattening. Its wild existence allows millions of visitors each year to be confronted with the inaccessible, and the canyon's beauty is made all the more sublime because its golden depths refuse to conform to our vast systems of seamless, mechanized transport.

Even while standing on the rim, the Grand Canyon reveals a place where human bodies maintain their meaning, where distances are still measured in footsteps or paddle strokes. If a tram were built here and ten thousand people a day could pay to ride to the confluence in fifteen minutes of cushioned comfort, discussing work or politics as they glide across previously unscalable canyon walls, they might arrive at these same coordinates where the blue waters of the Little Colorado have, for millennia, filled pilgrims of all kinds—from salt-gatherers to rafters—with wonder. But they would not be arriving in the same canyon. How could they? This place, defined by distance, realized by depth, would vanish.

W*e have our ovens.*

Down in the Imperial Valley where California dunes spill into Baja hills, the fence along the southern border stops and starts. In cities it grows into a wall of concrete and iron—solid, imposing, swathed in graffiti. Elsewhere, amid mazes of dirt two-tracks and blowing sand, it drops in height, more concerned with blocking vehicles than stopping humans. And for long stretches of rugged, remote terrain, it is reduced to a few strings of rusting barbed wire.

North of these wire breaks in the wall lie my nation's cooking fields, open-air ovens that bake away the rainfall and slow roast those who come walking up from the south—the brown bodies carrying bottles of water, suitcases, pink children's backpacks, the name of the town where relatives wait for them. The breaches in the fence are designed intentionally to funnel the newcomers into the desert, to thin the undesirables, the weakest and the unluckiest first, and to help ensure they'll be submissive workers when they arrive. The doorstep of our great meritocracy.

Some make it through. Others sit down in the shade of a creosote bush and never get up.

The desert often leaves skeletons intact, a sheath of leathered, vulture-plucked skin slowly shrinking around them until someone happens across their remains. For the fifteen years leading up to 2009, NAFTA was opening the flow of money (upward, as usual) and tightening the ratchet on the flow of banned bodies (which arrive from the south, for now). During those years, when authorities received reports of an unidentified corpse in Imperial County, the remains were often recovered and transported to the Terrace Park Cemetery in Holtville, California.

You can go there now, but only part of the cemetery is open to the public. Like the border, the graveyard is divided by a fence. On one side: green grass, elegant headstones, solemn visitors. On the other: yellow-brown dirt dotted with brick-sized markers. There, beyond the barbed wire where no sprinklers rotate, everyone has one of two names—John Doe or Jane Doe.

Imperial County has become more efficient since 2009. The dead are now collected from the desert and transported to a crematorium where they are converted to ash and smoke. The remains are then taken off the coast of California and scattered to the salt sea.

THE RIO

Spring 2018

Cool beer slides down my throat. We've just pushed away from a dirt boat ramp on the Rio Grande, boats loaded for a four-day trip. Eddy, an old college roommate, and Britt, a neighbor from Utah, float in inflatable kayaks beside me. We each have our own mountain of Busch—the seltzer of beers—weighing our boats down and causing them to scrape along the shallow riverbed. Upstream, the Rio Grande is dry for hundreds of miles, the Colorado snowmelt from its headwaters siphoned off to New Mexican fields and Texas cities until there is none left. The water that we're floating on is fed entirely by springs on the Mexican side of the line. Five minutes from the put-in we run aground. I wedge my open beer into a crack on the floor of the boat to keep it from spilling and push off the sandbar.

The wind picks up. We paddle against it for a while until I stop to pass out another round of St. Louis sparkling water. All three boats are immediately blown into some overhanging bushes on the south bank. No sirens sound, no lights flash. I get out to pee, and I'm in Mexico.

The following afternoon we stop again on the Mexican side to camp. We're still drinking as the warm river slips by. This thirst. I've traveled to the border three times this spring to interview activists along the line, but this week all I am planning to do is paddle. No deadlines, no investigations, no probing of our deadly immigration policies, I tell myself. But such a goal requires focus. For years now, updates from the border have rattled out of radio and television sets every day. These canyons are quiet, hardly a warzone, but I also know about the camps of children to our north, the loud demands that our government string a wall through this wilderness. A dry itch forms in the back of my throat, and I rise from the beach to go crack another beer.

Distraction arrives. Eddy assails us with stories about the five years he has just spent in Southeast Asia, where he at turns worked for the *Jakarta Post*, sat silent for months on end in Buddhist monasteries, and learned to kickbox on Thai beaches. He gives an accounting of his endless string of lovers, which slowly brings us back to Texas where he has come to study anthropology, and, when he can, to run rivers in Mexico.

When Eddy has exhausted himself with memories, tequila joins the rotation along with the beers. I bring out a desert book by Charles Bowden, which we take turns reading aloud. His words pour out into the silence, disjointed tales of border crossings, union battles, bats. The light turns dreamy and soft. The Rio is placid before us.

Dusk is falling when Bowden's words are interrupted by shouting in Spanish downstream. Eddy wanders toward the noise, barefoot and drunk. Britt and I follow. Two cowboys have roped a steer that is thrashing wildly in the brush. One of the men—maybe twenty years old with dusty clothes, a sweat-stained hat, and a thin black mustache floating above his brown lips—loops his rope around the trunk of a tamarisk tree and pulls tight. The lasso catches behind the steer's horns and its huge head comes forward until it is held in place against the stout tree trunk. A third cowboy, older with a tired, sun-leathered face, stands beside his horse and watches the young men work with quiet approval. Eddy approaches him in a flurry of Spanish, peppered with expletives and slurred vowels. The man smiles. Eddy gestures to the horse and then to himself and before anything can be said, Eddy's bare foot has gone through the stirrup and he's swung himself into the saddle.

The older cowboy seems unconcerned that a stranger has mounted his horse. The other cowboys finish or abandon their task with the steer—I can't tell which—and untie the ropes. The steer stomps off into the trees, snorting and shaking his head. Britt hands beers around to the three men. I talk to them in broken Spanish while Eddy makes obscene pronouncements from atop his perch.

"*Borracho?*" the older cowboy asks me, gesturing to Eddy and tipping his thumb back toward his mouth.

"*Claro,*" I reply.

Eddy reaches for the reins, still held lightly in the man's hands, and the cowboy gives them over. Giddy, Eddy sends a small kick into the horse's ribs and the man assists with a slap on its flank. It takes off, hooves sounding on the river cobbles, Eddy bouncing along.

One of the younger men crushes his beer can and tosses it in the bushes. "*Más?*" he asks. Britt leads them back to our camp where new cans are passed around.

The clatter of hooves, and Eddy comes bouncing back. He pulls the horse in beside us and attempts to swing out of the saddle, reins in hand, but as he comes off, his foot catches and he begins to fall backward. The only way he can stop himself from hitting the ground is to yank on the reins and all of us brace for the snap on the bit, the jolt through the horse's neck. But at the last moment he lets the leather strips slide through his fingers and he falls backward onto the dirt.

All the cowboys laugh.

It's 2014 in New Mexico. The clerk behind the counter of the computer store in Las Cruces greets him by name: Chuck, a writer known to the literary world as Charles Bowden. He is

here every two or three months and always with the same purchase—a new keyboard for his aging PC. Chuck sets the box on
the counter, and as the light flashes on the cash register screen, he
calculates the amount of fresh corn tortillas that could be bought
for the desperate who cross the border south of his house. Or
that money could have paid for yet another bottle of red wine to
be emptied into his ceramic mug one splash at a time.

But he has a job to do. He is a writer with angry fingers and
each day he must get his anger past that dancing cursor on his
monitor screen. This is a given, as essential as tortillas or wine.
The job requires fingers to connect with keys, and to get the cursor to move properly, the sound of the work must make noise.
It must sing through the house, *thwack, thwack, thwack*, and
after thousands of repetitive smacks in this rhythm, the springs
beneath their plastic sheaths break down and the letters cease to
appear on the screen and he needs to make another trip to the
computer store.

His teeth are falling out. He sleeps on a cot. There are pains
at night and he refuses to see a doctor or a dentist. In his bank account sit tens of thousands of dollars from a fellowship, earning
meager interest as they decay from inflation. The funds remain
untouched. That amount of money makes him uncomfortable.
He operates in freelance checks from magazines and twenty-
dollar bills. Most of his possessions and nearly all of this cash
have been given away to those who knock at his door.

For decades, he has been arguing with ghosts. Lately it has
been the ghost of his old friend Edward Abbey, the man who,
in his own fading years, promoted every one of Bowden's books
in letters to publishers, review journals, and conversations with
New York agents. Yet Bowden never got the praise and recogni-
tion Abbey began to suffer from near the end of his life. Bowden's
angry fingers produced dark books on drug wars, pedophiles,
CIA-sponsored torture—topics that many thought were best left
in darkness.

The new keyboard comes home and wine flows through the cup. The maddened compositions of another Charles—Charles Ives—scream noise out of his speakers as he thinks of Ed. Bowden sits on the porch and watches the hummingbirds flit around his feeders with erratic jerks as if to the music.

An essay is forming in Bowden's mind. It is for an Abbey anthology, meant to be another round of praise issued to his cantankerous old friend. But Bowden has never been one for simple praise. The essay, he decides, will be about Ed, Ives, and a fence in the sand down along the border.

Does he know that it will be one of his last? Bowden is sixty-nine. He has outlived Abbey, who died at sixty-two in 1989, by seven years. The twenty-first century is well underway and our collective obsession with progress, which enraged Abbey into writing his collected comedies about the destruction of the desert and the death of the free human, has only bloomed more fully since his death. Bowden has taken up where Abbey left off, documenting our steadfast advance through the ravaged, ever-innovative discontents of civilization.

He goes inside and positions his fingers on the clean, shiny keys.

The cowboys are staying. There is beer and the gringos are crazy. The younger two men head away from the river to build a fire. The older man, with the leathered face of a lifetime outside who says he's their uncle, spots the bottle of tequila among our gear and takes a deep slug. He lives a dozen miles upstream in the tiny Mexican town of Boquillas and runs a richer man's cattle through the canyons. For seven years, he lived in the United States. Good money and hard work. In halting English he tells us the story of those years.

"In Texas, worked concrete. Missouri, concrete. In Denver, we lived in a hotel. Cocaine and concrete. But now Boquillas." He shrugs. "In Mexico, fifteen dollars every day."

Tequila goes back to his lips.

There's a call from the mouth of a nearby side canyon, and the *tío*, the uncle, heads toward it. We follow. His nephews have built a fire of thin sticks, and the wind is pressing the flames flat against the ground as the coals roar red. The horses stand grazing on dry clumps of grass, and the firelight casts crazy shadows that swagger on the earth beyond their spindles of legs. Britt distributes a fresh round of Busch.

It's too windy here, so the nephews move up closer to the cliffs and build a second fire. They abandon the first and leave it ablaze, sparks skating toward the night. tío takes another slug from the bottle and offers it to his nephews who wave it off. They have wives waiting back in town. As do some of us gringos.

Somewhere out there, beyond the ring of firelight, there are families moving north. They come through Mexico, but, for the most part, they are no longer from Mexico. Net migration of Mexicans peaked in 2008, and a decade later is close to zero; just as many return home as enter the US.

Now, of the families that arrive, 80 percent are from three countries: El Salvador, Guatemala, and Honduras, all places where the American government has been meddling for over a century, at times propping up right-wing regimes and fueling gang violence. Some of the families who cross tonight have a plan for the morning. They will wave down a white car with green lettering and declare why they have come to a border patrol agent. Many refugees are running from persecution, state violence, or vicious husbands back home. They seek asylum. They fear death if they return. The agents will note the claim and ship off the new arrivals to a detention center to await judgment.

(Charles Ives speaks through the rapping of Chuck's keyboard: "Stand up and take your dissonance like a man.")

Claire, an attorney and high school classmate of mine, has been in one such center in Dilley, Texas, for six weeks. I speak to her on the phone, and she tells me she lives between doublewide trailers in oil country. She wakes early each day and pours bottled water into a coffee maker before she and her colleagues drive through pumpjack forests to work.

As seen from the sky, the landscape is slashed by so many strata of productivity. Interstates, two-lane highways, and country roads spool across the sparsely populated plains somewhere between Laredo and San Antonio. Between the roads, center-pivot irrigation systems etch circles on the earth beside rectangular fields of watermelon vines. White dots of dusty turnarounds for oil and gas trucks sit between compressor stations, fracking wells, and pipeline valves. This land has long been used with no regard for using it up, though the people here remain poor. But now there is a new industry in town. One that brings lawyers. And security guards. And news coverage. The country's largest immigrant detention facility for families is tucked at the end of a gravel road beyond an unmarked highway intersection.

Claire and her companions work pro bono, and each morning when they arrive at Dilley, they undergo a full security screening. She has learned to conceal a couple of crayons for the detained children in the cartons of coffee she brings inside. If the security guard seems interested in searching her things, she'll ask him about his favorite taco shop while her coffee is being x-rayed. His eyes dart off the screen as he gives directions to the stand and describes the flavor of the tacos *al pastor*. The coffee emerges from the other side of the machine, the crayons still concealed. Crayons here are contraband. Management says they pose a vandalization threat to the privately run, for-profit jail.

Claire's tale sharpens and settles on a single day. The screening ate up fifteen minutes, but her smuggling operation has not been discovered. She is through. Her brisk steps crunch as she crosses the gravel lot to another modular. Beyond, a line of temporary units containing 2,400 beds stretch away into the boiling Texas heat. Triple razor wire fences surround the facility. No men are detained here, just hundreds of women and their children waiting to tell their stories and have their asylum claims processed.

Claire waits in a small room. She'll be here as long as she can, usually twelve hours, meeting with twelve or more refugee women. Her job is to explain the asylum process and to help the women prepare for their asylum interviews. The stories, and how they are told, mean everything. To be granted asylum under US law you must be able to prove persecution or a "well-founded fear" of persecution back home.

The first clients have arrived. The mother is small, under five feet, with very dark skin. A young boy clings to her leg. Claire greets them. She tries to make it clear she is here to help; this is not an ICE interview, but a safe place to talk freely. The woman speaks Spanish, though it is clear she's indigenous and also speaks a tongue that's been used on this continent much longer. She came from Guatemala.

The clock is ticking. Claire has an hour to get the stories out. A crayon emerges from its hiding place and goes to the little boy along with a yellow legal pad. He sits quietly—they are always so quiet, she thinks—and he starts to scribble.

The lines he draws across the paper begin to resemble the view of Dilley, Texas, from above. Circles, winding streams, dots. And underneath his marks, the straight, printed lines on the paper race away like roads to nowhere.

Dissonance. Trade crosses borders freely while the walls go up before the fleeing and starving who arrive from the south. Bowden writes in 2014 about an Abbey essay from the 1980s, which Abbey had called one of his favorites. It's entitled "Immigration and Liberal Taboos."

Abbey's point is straightforward. There are too many people in America, and our wildernesses, our non-human neighbors, and even our cities cannot take any more. So Abbey comes out and hangs a sign on our border because, he says, no one else will do it. *No Vacancy*, it reads. In the essay, Abbey calls the newest arrivals to our country "hungry, ignorant, unskilled, and culturally-morally-genetically impoverished." Everybody is afraid to demand we build a damn wall because "the conservatives love their cheap labor; the liberals love their cheap cause. (Neither group, you will notice, ever invites the immigrants to move into their homes. Not into their homes!)" We need more security, Abbey says, bring our troops home and station them at the border.

Missouri, concrete. El Paso, concrete.

Abbey lectures from the pulpit. "We have nothing to gain and everything to lose by allowing the old boat to be swamped." In the swarming cities, he tells us, human freedom is the first victim. And in the countryside? When was the country overbooked from the point of view of the red-spotted toad, the peregrine, the bison? We're full, we're full. Easy words if you're speaking from behind the wall. But Abbey is being honest to his own dispositions. He takes issue not so much with the threat of violence or the theft of jobs—those infractions our wall-builders clamor on about today—no, not that; Abbey has a bone to pick with the mothers. The women giving birth, the brown women. The itch in the throat. Bowden feels he needs to speak up.

Pfft, Abbey cracks a Schlitz in his study.

Pop, the cork comes out of Bowden's wine.

"*Quieres?*" Tío passes me the tequila.

Bowden has one hand on the cup and another on Abbey's book, which contains the immigration essay. He's living in the New Mexico desert twenty years after Abbey made these remarks. The border, a couple dozen miles from his house, is now both secured with walls and leaky as a sieve.

The book goes facedown and Bowden walks to his computer. *Thwack, thwack, thwack.* Hours drift by, and he pauses from the tapping of his keys only when he hears another tapping at his door. "Christ, there is that knocking," he writes. "She is a young woman. She has a child, a husband with diabetes. She has no job. In Mexico, her sister-in-law got on the wrong side of the wrong people, and if she goes back they will kill her, her brother, his wife, their child."

Abstract from that moment, that person, that knocking, and Abbey's rantings against overpopulation can appear reasonable. But today Bowden issues a challenge: "Look into the eyes of a frightened Mexican girl in the desert trying to reach her people in some small town in America, and all the clever words fall into the dust."

Bowden invites her inside and feeds her.

Kleenex. Claire brings in cases every day. In the interviews the women seldom sob, but there are always quiet tears along with the stories. *Describe your well-founded fear.* And even when the weeping stops the noses are always running. It's 110 degrees outside, but in these trailers the children shiver. Everyone has a cough, a dripping nose. Many lean over the toilet multiple times a day and retch. Claire sips from a bottle of water between sessions. As do the guards and administrative staff. The women and children drink from the tap. The water has an odd smell. It has been pulled from an aquifer that's been punctured for decades by the thirsty straws of the oil and gas wells above. The prison has nearly doubled the population of the town and has strained the capacity of the wastewater treatment plant. The tap water is almost certainly contaminated, the attorneys agree, but they do not know with what; they have other, more immediate work to do. They just know that for the detainees, there are many trips to the toilet. And boxes and boxes of Kleenex.

A new woman sits before Claire. She is twenty-eight years old and rolls a string of plastic rosary beads between her fingers. Her daughter is five and has a crayon in her hand. Claire looks the mother in the eye and gives her a tissue.

The story begins. The woman owned a nail salon in Granada, Nicaragua, and made good money, or good enough. A few months before she was locked in Dilley, President Daniel Ortega, the one-time Marxist guerilla turned pro-austerity capitalist, proposed cuts to the people's pensions held by the Nicaraguan Institute for Social Security, known under its Spanish acronym INSS. Chants broke out in the streets. Cars were lit on fire in Managua and the people began protesting outside the salon owner's shop. She took a scrap of cardboard, wrote in block letters *SOS INSS*, and joined the protest.

There was a knock at her door the following day. Men with dark bags under their eyes crowded on the step and one held up a photo on the screen of a phone. It was of her and her cardboard sign. The man with the phone did all the talking. He praised the government and expressed great concern for her daughter's safety. Behind him, three other men licked their lips.

They left, but she did not. The bars were locked across the windows of her salon for a week. The protests continued and the military set up roadblocks around her neighborhood and trucks were stopped from making deliveries. Food prices went up. Her husband crept through the barricades one night to get rice. He never returned. She took her daughter, a bit of cash, and headed north.

Now she is in Dilley. Other mothers in the prison arrived earlier in the summer. Their children were stripped from them and thrown into cages of their own and told not to touch the other children. They huddled under foil space blankets among the wails of the hundreds like them. Phone calls were allowed every so often but were scratchy and the connections dropped. Another detainee in Dilley that Claire knew was reunited with her child after two months apart. Their first day outside of the prison together, the girl, hardly more than a toddler, suffered the first seizure of her life. Claire witnessed the ambulances arriving for the girl at a bus stop in a Texas city.

⌒

It is December 1968 and Hannah Arendt, the refugee philosopher, is in Washington, DC.

Months ago, Martin Luther King Jr. was gunned down and the riots swept across Chicago, Baltimore, the nation's capital. In Vietnam, more than one million displaced people are on the move. Arendt prepares her notes. She is of German-Jewish descent and fled for Paris in 1933 before settling in New York. France was immobilized in May of 1968, and seemed to teeter on the cusp of some envisioned freedom, but that has passed and now Arendt gives a lecture on collective responsibility. Morality is tied to the self, she says, our guilt and actions and conscience. But each of us also shares a political responsibility, not for ourselves but for the nation. Belonging to a community ties us to a shared history so that "we are always held responsible for the sins of our fathers as we reap the rewards of their merits." History cannot be undone; our responsibilities can be shirked but not dissolved. She is clear on this. But, she admits, there is one exception:

> [T]he twentieth century has created a category of men who were truly outcasts, belonging to no internationally recognizable community whatever, the refugees and stateless people, who indeed can not be held politically responsible for anything. Politically, regardless of their group or individual character, they are the absolutely innocent ones; and it is precisely this absolute innocence that condemns them to a position outside, as it were, of mankind as a whole.

The families who come from the south tonight and every night will be torn apart at the gates of the American dream tomorrow. What responsibility do they have for the gangs on one end of the journey or the cages on the other? To be a citizen of a nation or of humanity requires being responsible, in some manner at least, for the actions of the whole. But to be without a state, to be a citizen of no nation, says Arendt, is to be subhuman, to risk desert crossings and having your children ripped from your arms. Before a refugee can even fight for their freedom or dignity, they must, in one of Arendt's famous articulations, struggle for the very "right to have rights." Those that survive the open-air ovens find their way into the camps. For what crime? For being stateless. For running.

Arendt lights a cigarette and leans on the lectern. The stateless ones. The refugees. "Actually, they are the only totally nonresponsible people," she says in her stern German accent, "and while we usually think of responsibility, especially collective responsibility, as a burden and even as a kind of punishment, I think it can be shown that the price paid for collective nonresponsibility is considerably higher."

I sip my Busch as the cowboys fall silent and we all stare into the fire. Deep in the flames, I see the rotating balloon of a cement truck in Denver spewing its thick sludge down the metal chute. Concrete and cocaine. Tío is waiting with a shovel to direct that flow into the forms of a foundation.

For three summers during college, I worked at a camp for high schoolers striving to become first-generation college students. The participants' families were mostly recent arrivals from south of our southern border, and many of the students were undocumented though they crossed the line as toddlers or infants and could remember living in no country but the United States. We'd sift through college applications, and I'd assist with the essays they were writing to scholarship funds and university admissions offices. "Describe a time you faced adversity," the questionnaire would demand. And the students' stories would pour out. Of babysitting younger siblings while Mom worked two jobs. Of watching older siblings drop out of high school to work at construction sites so their little sister could stay in school and apply to college. Of being called *illegal* and *alien* and *wetback* and *beaner*, and being told there was no point in setting sights higher than scrubbing floors.

One of my fellow counselors came up through the program as a high school student and was, like me, a junior in college. She was undocumented, and all her life was poured into studying pre-med at a private university that she was attending on a full-ride scholarship. Her warm eyes kept flitting away when she talked as if she couldn't let that most important thing out of her sight: her future. I asked her on a date and we went hiking a few times. We kissed on a boulder of red sandstone and she told me through a smile that she could never achieve anything but total perfection. Her family's dreams were sunk into her success. The government could deport them for any infraction.

That fall she was back in school wrapping up a double major while working part-time at a lab, and she wouldn't return my calls. I'd get a text. She was too busy, no time for walks or sandstone. But there was an additional reason: we lived in different worlds. I, a white boy, could stumble. And more than once, I did—like when I was pulled over for driving with no lights at eighteen. I had just left the liquor store where my friend had bought a case of beer thanks to a fake ID held out with shaking hands, and the adrenaline made me forget about my headlights as we pulled away. The beer was in the backseat, but the cop politely ignored it. I got off with a warning. Yes, I could fall. She could never so much as slip.

The refugees keep arriving. They come across the Rio, wading through the warm water with children in their arms. It is shallow, but if they lose their balance, it's over. Many do not know how to swim. Each year, the border patrol finds bloated bodies floating facedown in canals and the river. Slipping is not an option, but sometimes even remaining upright is not enough.

In California, ICE arrests a man who is driving his wife to the hospital to give birth. He is deported. Abbey grumbles about birth control for the people he is no longer allowed to call *wetbacks* in a book dedicated to three of his five white children.

Bowden pours another glass of wine and thinks of the migrant mother he sent off that morning with a roll of his cash tucked into her shoe. He writes:

> The wall now rising on the Mexican border is a comfort to police agents and small children, the only two groups that might see it as a solution to overpopulation, resource limits, poverty, and global warming. It will buy some votes for politicians, it will create some misery for migrating humans and wildlife. But it will not alter the future. When you live on the line and see up close the murder of dreams, you find that facts transcend logic. The millions here are not going home. And the time is past that the world can be kept at bay by a wall.

The nephews are ready to go home. They try to wrangle their drunk tío onto his horse, but Eddy is distracting him. He has spotted a rifle slung through the saddle and he wants to shoot it. The tío is laughing, telling him guns are illegal in Mexico and that maybe he'll have to shoot us if we tell. Eddy is insistent. He gestures to the fire as his target, now burned down to a circle of coals and ash in a five-foot diameter. Tío relents. He clicks off the safety, chambers a bullet, and hands the rifle to Eddy, who dances on his bare feet with glee. Taking aim, he pulls the trigger. The crack echoes off the canyon walls and fades into empty space.

It is Claire's last interview of the day and in comes another woman, also small, also dark-skinned. She is from Honduras, in a city where the boundaries of two rival gangs rub against each other, emitting sparks of constant violence. Her daughter, at ten, is older than most of the children in these cages. She looks out from black eyes deep with horrors. It hasn't been six months since she was walking home from school with two friends when gang members, not much older than the girls, came around the corner. Guns were pulled from the waistbands of jeans. The daughter ran. Two blasts rang out and her friends were no longer running beside her. Perhaps it was retribution for some infraction of a family member. The motivation was never clear, Claire is told, but the ten-year-old was a witness to this crime and the gangs knew it.

The daughter knew it too, and when she came spilling through the door of her home, all sweat and screams, she told her mother what had happened, and the mother made a fatal mistake. She asked for help. There had been a double murder, and her daughter's life was in danger. What was there to do but believe there would be some justice? With nervous fingers, she punched in the number for the police station.

The response was prompt. In fifteen minutes, a knock at the door. The stories so often have this knock. The mother answered and the boys outside wore tattoos instead of uniforms. They told her she had been summoned. There was no choice now but to meet her fate. They led her to a prison where a local gang boss had set up shop. He was in jail, yes, but the prison guards, like the cops, were his employees. The cell was his office. The interrogation required few words; the leader already had all the information he needed. Yet she could not leave. While she was held, dozens of men entered the gang leader's office, and they each forced their way inside. The raping went on for twelve hours.

The Kleenex dabs, and Claire wipes her own eyes. The mother's soft Spanish words flow from her tongue and land on the lines of Claire's yellow notepad.

"I died," the mother from Honduras says simply. "They killed me in that cell."

She went home from the prison and strung a rope from the ceiling. But before she could tie the noose and slip it around her neck, another knock. It was her daughter this time. That was all it took. Death could not come yet. The rope was still hanging when they left that very night to flee north. Three other children, ages two, five, and seven, stayed with the father as mother and daughter, witnesses to the crimes, boarded a bus to Mexico and traveled to the Texas line. If they return, if their refugee claim fails and they are deported, it is certain what will happen.

There is fear, sure. But the asylum officer will want to know if it is well-founded.

A federal court ruling sets the limit for child detention at three weeks. In Dilley, where Claire takes down stories on her pad, the compound is run by CoreCivic, a publicly traded corporation that makes $1.7 billion in annual revenue managing private prisons and immigrant detention centers. While Claire meets with twelve mothers a day, there are 1,500 women and children behind the razor wire. They are almost always detained for the full three-week limit before being released to process their claims or being deported back to the violence of the south. The longer each woman and child stays in the camps, the more money is funneled to CoreCivic's board and shareholders. Lobbyists press to extend the three-week limit and bolster revenue. The rules will be changed soon enough. But even with the limit, Dilley rakes in $13 million of taxpayer money each month.

If the refugees survive the desert, they are spared from the heat. The cages are concrete and cold. In the middle of summer, one eighteen-month-old child comes down with fevers in Dilley where the air conditioning is set so low the migrants call it the *hielera*, the icebox. Like many of the children, she has a respiratory infection but receives no medical treatment. Six weeks after being released with her family, the girl dies.

Bowden strikes the keys and words appear: "You find that facts transcend logic."

Edward Abbey is going to break down liberal taboos. To say what needs to be said but what everyone is too timid to speak out loud. "It occurs to some of us that perhaps ever continuing industrial and population growth is not the true road to human happiness, that simple gross quantitative increase of this kind creates only more pain, dislocation, confusion, and misery. In which case it might be wise for us as American citizens to consider calling a halt to the mass influx of even more millions of hungry, ignorant, unskilled, and culturally-morally-genetically impoverished people." The world is overpopulated, the habitats shrink, the fuel is burned, the climate warms, yes, but there's just one hitch with Abbey's solution: the population, every last bit of it, consists of people.

Claire's notepad fills up. The cowboys mount their horses in the dark. I give Tío the bottle for the long ride home, and he thanks me. The dark, slim woman from Honduras and her daughter who witnessed the murders sit for their asylum interview and pass the first round. They are dropped at a bus station in San Antonio. Next will come paperwork, legal fees, a hearing to see if they'll be granted asylum.

Bowden is looking at birds along a creek. A Central American man stumbles out of the brush. Bowden feeds him, drives him around a border patrol checkpoint, and slips one hundred dollars into his backpack. And again a knock comes at the door. Claire hands the Honduran woman a scrap of paper with her number and says she will keep helping. Arendt lights another cigarette, pauses in her speech on collective responsibility, and thinks of the faces that disappeared into the European ovens when her home country became overpopulated all those years ago.

Abbey moves, Bowden counters, Ives' music streams from the stereo, the keys *thwack*. "Look into the eyes of a frightened

Mexican girl in the desert, and all the clever words fall into the dust."

The cowboys are gone, and I'm in my sleeping bag staring up at the wild swirl of stars along the canyon's black skyline. I think of my own mother who taught English for years at the public elementary school, mostly to children whose parents were from Central America or Mexico, some of them with documents, some without. These students, the first generation in America, were the people Abbey was talking about, the ones who draw the jeers at the political rallies now. The catalysts of the overpopulation problem, the future takers of jobs. The Colorado where we lived was growing more crowded, the roads buzzing with traffic, the fourteeners swarming like anthills with hikers, the fracking wells going in to feed the growing demands of our homes and automobiles. So what's the answer? Deportations! Sterilizations! Cages! My mom kneels before a third grader and helps him sound out a word on the page. She sees faces, not population; children, not pests.

When I wasn't working at the summer camp for the students applying to college, I took a landscaping job in Aspen. I was nineteen and skinny when I first arrived at the company, and the owner took one look at me before I was assigned to the women's crew. I was the only American-born member of the team, and as far as I knew the only citizen. We didn't talk about documents. But I was hired because I was the one with a driver's license, and I drove a big white company pickup along the Roaring Fork River each morning, forty-five minutes by highway, until we'd park in the driveway of some towering mansion, the remote-controlled shades drawn across the windows swirling in dark light like oil slicks on the sea. The house would be empty for fifty weeks every year, heated in the winter, cooled in the summer, the lawn immaculate.

Bowden calls out Abbey for his laziness in his immigration essay: you blamed the poorest, Bowden says, you scapegoated those with the least recourse to defense. I want to chime in. Abbey, you were never one for letting bold plans deter you, so why didn't you call for the obscenely rich to be fined and then deported? The estates of their third homes sprawl through what was lynx habitat, their chartered jets wait down on the runway, burning fuel. If you want change, why not seize their property and give it back to the mountain lion, the grizzly bear, the banana slug, as you were fond of saying? Would the response be different if it were their children in cages, sleeping under tinfoil blankets and drinking water that emits the vapors of their parents' secret, proprietary fracking fluid formulas? And if that is unsettling to contemplate, then it's time to think about why. Is it because the billionaires' children, like your own, are mostly fair-haired?

And Bowden, you were right to challenge Abbey when he erred, but maybe you were never able to think big enough. You always took it down to the particulars, the face before you, the knock at the door, as is necessary to check and balance any grand ethical rules. But if we only ever respond to the face in front of us, we've already given up on the possibilities for a different world, which require a more ambitious vision. Those who would lock children in cages are organized; there's solidarity between the private prisons and the bulldozers that clear new roads along the border. We can no longer respond only as individuals. Ed's sugar in gas tanks didn't exactly work, no matter how fun it was. And Chuck, the tortillas you pressed into the hands of the frightened girl along with a prepaid calling card and the crumple of cash, that was everything to her, but now there is another girl at your door, and you're not around to answer it any longer. The world will not be kept at bay by a wall, but nor will it be improved through isolation. The people in the streets chant ¡El pueblo *unido!* Arendt understood that having a code of ethics without participating in a collective, political sense of responsibility was a farce. Without it comes fatalism, the despair of Bowden and the ranting of Abbey, and I feel that same fatalism coursing through my veins. But things can change, they have to change, and when they do there's no telling how fast it will come.

I was camped in the blizzards of Standing Rock where a tent city was erected in the path of pipelines. In the camps, wounds were being healed. Counselors offered their services to addicts and abuse survivors. Cooks distributed mountains of donated food. I was there in a lull between the militarized private security and police responses to the protests, on the day when ten thousand people stood hand in hand in a great ring around the camps. At the very moment when our section of the circle was completed, a runner came down the line bearing word from Washington: Obama had stopped the pipeline. And even though the incoming president would reverse course and the pipeline would go through a few months later, that gathering was not fruitless. It has spurred a thousand other acts of resistance, and since it was born in community, in solidarity, the next Standing Rock will be even bigger and harder for the powerful to tamp down.

The wall will not change the future, says Bowden. But those tearing at the wall still could.

On this night, the migrants crossing are still scattered and broken, as are my thoughts. There is too much Abbey and Bowden in me. I'm another one of the men drunk on ideas and booze. I seek escape and silence. I drift down to the burning border, not to help with sugar or tortillas or crayons, but to float into this severed wilderness canyon between two nations and to see what it has to offer me and my own private melancholy. But wind-beaten faces emerge in the dusk, light a fire, and speak of pouring concrete.

The children sit on the floor making their crazy drawings. The mothers cry silent tears as the tissues float from the boxes and soak up their stories. They run their fingers over plastic rosary beads and wipe the dripping noses of their children. The tap water smells, the pumpjacks groan, the power lines hum, the air conditioners rage.

Bowden, sitting alone in his kitchen, fills his mug and toasts to Ed.

Tio takes another pull, and I reach over for the bottle.

The sparks are flying. Anyone who doesn't feel the heat is already asleep. On the banks of the Rio Grande, an ember leaps from the fire and lands in a patch of dry grass. Up it roars in a crown of light that pushes against the darkness.

I t is 1912 and the waters are rising. Snowmelt roars down polished slate canyons on Washington's Olympic Peninsula, but five miles from the sea it pools against the wall of a new dam. The moss-slung trees in the reservoir bed have been hauled away, leaving only a basin of raw stumps. As the lake fills for the first time, they slip beneath water one by one.

Nestled in the clear-cut is a gray boulder with two round depressions on its surface, usually full of rainwater. The depressions are named after the coiled baskets woven from cedar roots by the local Lower Elwha Klallam people and made watertight with pine pitch or beeswax. For centuries, they gathered at the rock. Teenagers have crouched by it for days, seeking visions and direction. Elders sing tales of its power. It was from this rock, they recall, that their people emerged in the earliest times into this wet world of dark forests and blue rivers pouring into an angry sea. The rock is often strewn with offerings—salmon, weavings, prayers. With heavy rains or during the spring runoff, the rock is submerged, and its crown of gifts is accepted by the floods.

Rock, river, salmon, sea, people—each of these sustains the others. Or they once did. Things are unraveling. Construction on the dam began in 1910, and now the reservoir is coming to drown the coiled-basket rock. But before the rock goes under, a rupture tears through the base of the dam. Water explodes thick brown from the foundation, and the reservoir drains in a great rush.

When the flood recedes in the channel below, thousands of salmon are strung in the trees like new offerings to a new god. The god of the whites.

The dam builders have no patience for delays. Mats of fir trees are brought in and used to patch the breach. Concrete is forced into the foundation. The repairs hold. A year later, stagnant water creeps up the sides of the coiled-basket rock, pours into the depressions, and sinks it under shimmering depths for good.

THE DAM

T his was a stupid idea. My knees tremble as I lower myself to the ground beneath the weight of a pack that bulges with camping gear, drysuit, paddle, lifejacket, deflated packraft, and a week's worth of food. But I don't dare complain as I watch David strain to lean his load against a tree without losing his balance. Tied to his back with a tangle of black straps is an unwieldy sixty-pound whitewater kayak stuffed with another fifty pounds of gear.

"We probably should have looked at the map," he says, not for the first time.

I nod and try to flash a smile, though I'm certain if I'd looked at a map I wouldn't be here now. After so many journeys to remote rivers, I know better than to haul a full paddling kit deep into the backcountry. As a child of recovering backpackers turned raft guides, I was trained at an early age to hate two things: packs heavy with gear and river-killing dams. So when I heard the Elwha River—which is flowing somewhere in the valley far below us—was the site of the largest dam removal project in history, I knew I had to go. But I also knew I'd have to trick myself to get there; I avoided maps or any real plan until I'd arrived on the Olympic Peninsula and it was too late to turn back.

121

Now as I rest on the edge of this soft duff trail between ferns and old-growth cedars, the only sensible option is to keep going. Our goal is to trace the Elwha from its alpine source in the Olympic Mountains to the Pacific Ocean, a length of forty-five miles. But we first have to hike thirty miles upstream to get to the Elwha's source.

I feel out of place in this temperate rainforest where I can see no rock. The peninsula gets twelve feet of rain per year and the surface of the earth is still blanketed in green, even though this year the area is suffering a severe drought. The rivers I know best flow through a desert that gets about six *inches* of annual precipitation and the trees don't grow far from the water's edge. In that desert, dams store water for thirsty Southwestern farms and cities—precious snowmelt distributed to thousands of lawns, urinals, and lettuce fields. Here, near the Pacific coast, the air is sticky, the forest claustrophobic. The Elwha and Glines Canyon Dams, completed in 1913 and 1927, were built for a different purpose than water storage; they were designed to fuel a logging boom. It worked. The river was directed through turbines. The electricity powered saw blades that ripped through the trunks of old-growth trees and turned them into marketable lumber. The economy in the nearby logging town of Port Angeles flourished.

As the dams brought in a rush of settlement to nearby towns, they delivered a near-fatal blow to the longest residents of the area, the Lower Elwha Klallam community. For centuries, salmon had been the major staple of the Klallam peoples' diet. The tribe constructed elaborate weirs built of fir and cedar boughs, which directed fish toward anglers' nets. Each spring, tribal members would tow elk bone hooks on kelp lines from the back of their dugout canoes in the bay. As the anglers hauled in a giant, thrashing chinook, the other paddlers would lean over the opposite side of the canoe to keep it from flipping. In 1855, the tribe had been forced to sell four hundred thousand acres of land, including the Elwha River, for three hundred thousand dollars. They'd been told they needed to relocate to a reservation one hundred miles away, and those who stayed—squatters in their own homeland—survived almost exclusively on salmon.

Then came the dams. The Elwha Dam, built just five miles from the sea, cut off the vast majority of spawning grounds and salmon populations plummeted. The Elwha was one of a few rivers in the Pacific Northwest that supported all five species of Pacific salmon and its historic runs consisted of an estimated four hundred thousand fish. When the Elwha Dam and the Glines Canyon Dam went in, that number fell to about three thousand fish. Meanwhile, the population of the Lower Elwha Klallam Tribe, once several thousand strong, dropped to just sixty-seven. Through all of this, the people remembered the river that had been lost and told stories of the old balance. And as the salmon circled at the foot of the Elwha Dam for a century, they held within their bodies intricate maps of saltwater, rapids, and spawning beds high in the mountains.

From the trail, the river is obscured by the forest, but I know that right now salmon are nosing upstream into tributaries they could have forgotten. Creation pushes on. As we rise to shoulder our loads again, gnats buzz in my ears.

Also with David and me is Eliza, a friend who drove up from Oregon to join our hike. She walks ahead of us and ignores our griping. Eliza knows how to be patient with overwhelmed people struggling in the backcountry; in the summers, she works as a wilderness therapy leader for at-risk youth, and regularly spends fifty days sea canoeing in Alaska. She feels less comfortable in whitewater, and she decided not to bring a boat for this trip. When it came time to divvy up the group gear, however, she packed more than her share.

We waddle up the trail with all the efficiency of backpacking seals. Thick forest surrounds us most of the way, but every so often we glimpse the far side of the valley where old clear-cuts have turned the slope to patchwork.

The Lower Elwha Klallam people were eventually granted a small reservation near the mouth of the Elwha, but land meant little without the salmon that had sustained their people beyond memory. The tribe built a hatchery. It helped stabilize populations, though the salmon raised in the holding tanks were weaker and more susceptible to disease than wild fish. The pens were crowded and fish had to be pumped full of antibiotics.

By the mid-1980s, the aging dams were only partially powering Port Angeles. So tribal leaders made a bold demand: the dams should come down and natural salmon runs should be restored. Indigenous activists and environmentalists persisted through years of controversy and delays, and in 2001, the federal government was able to purchase the dams. It took another decade before the legal groundwork to remove them was in place and the funds, some $325 million in all, were secured. Only then did the demolition begin.

Conservation groups and tribal officials praised the removal project. Robert Elofson, a Lower Elwha Klallam elder and the tribe's Director of River Restoration, told reporters that the dam removal was "the number one project for the tribe for many, many years . . . I'm very proud of it." But he acknowledged recovery wouldn't happen all at once. "There has not, for one hundred years, been anything more than five miles upstream. So [while the salmon] are moving up, it's happening slowly."

I hadn't talked to any locals about what had happened in their backyard until we were packing our boats at the trailhead. Two silver-haired couples stepped out of a sedan and told us this was their first trip to Glines Canyon since the dams were blasted apart. I asked one of them, a mustachioed white man in suspenders, what he thought of the removal.

He chuckled. "I'll tell you, I've got mixed feelings. I worked for thirty years at the mill in Port Angeles that owned these dams. I was dead set against the project when they started—seemed like a waste of money—but now after seeing it, I'm not so sure. They did a beautiful job. It sure is great to see the river again."

That night we camp in a grove of old-growth Douglas firs. The low branches of nearby hemlocks droop with stringy moss. Just beyond the fire ring, the Elwha rushes by. It's so clear that when it settles in deep pools, the river glows a bright blue, appearing backlit in the otherwise dark forest. We eat bowls of cheese and instant mashed potatoes and shuffle off to lay our sleeping pads on beds of pine needles. I click on my headlamp as daylight fades and slide a thin set of pages bound with duct tape from a Ziploc bag. When backpacking, especially with the excessive gear required for a paddling trip, I treat my reading material like my food: the denser the better, peanut butter and philosophy. For the Elwha trip, I used a pocket knife to slice a section from a crumbling paperback, a lecture on technology by German philosopher Martin Heidegger. I also have a xeroxed copy of an earlier version of the same lecture. I'm hoping Heidegger can help me understand what has happened here on the Elwha.

Heidegger spent his life thinking about being. Edward Abbey once remarked that it took Heidegger "a mere seventeen volumes" to say "Let Being be," and in this essay Heidegger seems to be proving Abbey's point. He argues that modern technology refuses to let being be; he calls it a "plundering drive" that turns all that exists in the world—from colonized continents right down to electrons—into fodder for technological progress. For Heidegger, technology isn't a set of tools but a "way of revealing," and in technological society, the vexing and beautiful mess of creation, all that *is*, appears to us as resources. "The earth now reveals itself as a coal mining district," he writes, "the soil as a mineral deposit," and the river as a "power supplier."

This way of revealing is so pervasive, it's like sunlight falling through a forest; we may notice the tree trunks and ferns in the understory, but it's easy to forget the light itself is responsible for revealing the forest to our eyes. Even when conservationists try to escape technology's grasp by setting aside wilderness or by halting development, they often do so from within this world-view. Canyons appear as scenic resources, mountains as recreational assets, wilderness areas as storage units for something called biodiversity. And we now have a name that Heidegger may have anticipated for employees: human resources.

I roll over and listen to the Elwha murmuring in the darkness on its way to the sea. As a paddler, I have a reflexive dislike for reservoirs, but that doesn't mean I can imagine a world without them. It's easy for me to grasp why the dams were built in the first place, why power and electricity have always been irresistible. I can understand why settlers cut through forests because when I see a river I too want to consume it until it's a part of me. I want it to wait there on standby until I'm ready to paddle it, just like the dam managers who could spin up the turbines as needed to meet demand at the mills.

The Klallam, like many Northwest tribes, practice the potlatch ceremony, where a prominent community member might spend years amassing food and wealth in order to, over the course of a few days, give everything away. Today, the America that I live in is by and large a society of hoarders—there is a surge of power pent up behind every outlet and light socket. But once in a while the dams come down. Could the freeing of the Elwha be a new kind of potlatch, the relinquishing of the technological for the wild? I click off my headlamp and fall asleep in minutes.

Dawn breaks cloudless and cool. Looking at a map over breakfast, we calculate that we're still twenty miles from the river's alpine source. Beaten from yesterday's long trek and dreading the trail to come, David and I begin to rationalize. We're here to paddle, not hike. And as paddlers, why not shoot for the navigable source of the river as opposed to the hydrological one? We forge our own rules, after all, and following the entire river was something we'd decided on from the comfortable chambers of our emails prior to the trip.

The abrasions on my shoulders, raw from the drybag straps, stick to the inside of my shirt. Shooting for the navigable source sounds reasonable and much easier. So we decide to leave the bulk of our gear and David's kayak behind and, carrying only our packrafts and lunch, strike out for a point we've picked on the map about twelve miles upstream. From there, David and I plan to paddle back to camp and Eliza will return on foot, arriving in time for dinner.

We hike up-river all day until the water is jammed with logs and too low to float our packrafts. Though it's late afternoon, turning back here at the "navigable source" now seems like a copout. The Elwha's true source is only eight miles up the trail. Again, we rationalize. Our tents, sleeping bags, and warm clothes are sitting with our food back in last night's camp. Continuing means a cold night without shelter and a long hungry day tomorrow.

"It's been a while since I've done something really hard," Eliza reasons, and with that we continue the slog.

With evening setting in, we drop our bags in a clearing and gather firewood. David lights a fire. We move only to push the unburned ends of sticks into the crackling pile of pine. For dinner we eat the last bites of our peanut butter sandwiches.

Eliza reaches in her daypack. "Don't say I didn't come prepared," she says, producing a crooked joint.

Sitting back against a log, we pull smoke into our lungs and let it swirl up through the boughs overhead where it mixes with the campfire haze. The temperature drops. David and I struggle into our drysuits, full-body Gore-Tex coveralls sealed with rubber gaskets around the neck and wrists, and we give our raincoats to Eliza. My friends soon nod off. The mixture of weed and hunger begins to carve strange channels through my mind.

I start to worry about robots.

A few weeks earlier, I'd read a piece about artificial intelligence by techno-optimist and Google executive Ray Kurzweil. His basic premise is that technology is accelerating along an exponential curve. It took tens of thousands of years for humans to advance from fire-starting to agriculture, then thousands more to get to the Industrial Revolution. But recently, only a few dozen years have been needed for what would have been considered supercomputers by 1970s standards to start buzzing in everyone's pockets. Extrapolating out from this trend, Kurzweil predicts that artificial intelligence—technology that is able to improve upon its own design without human intervention—will soon be developed. When this happens, even the most advanced problems of engineering such as travel at light speed will be solved within decades. Nano printers will be able to manufacture any material from raw molecules and the problems of resource scarcity will disappear. Human consciousness will merge completely with machine consciousness—our brains downloaded to some advanced version of computer chips—and death will no longer be tied to the frailties of the body. (Kurzweil glosses over why, at this point, machines would want or need to keep human consciousness around.) And in the final *coup de grace* to human limitations, this intelligent machinery will expand throughout the entire universe to harness "every atom" for its own ends.

Heidegger's assertion that technology reveals being as a resource is confirmed in Kurzweil's work. In fact, Kurzweil takes the technological mode of ordering to its utmost conclusion; even the great unusable reaches of outer space will become resources to feed our civilization.

The thought of robots eating their way across the universe makes my head swell like a balloon. My skull expands outward, consuming fire, friends, and forest. I feel it push out past planets, suns, and galaxies. Me, us, everywhere. Why wait for robots? The universe begs to be colonized, and daydreams move faster than light.

A century after Freud remarked that humans have been continually thrown from the center of things, first with Copernicus, then with Darwin, then with psychoanalysis where even our own rationality is called into question, Silicon Valley boosters have reclaimed the anthropocentric throne. They want to impregnate the entire universe with our consciousness, and if you're everywhere, who cares where the center is? All of this, Heidegger might say, was contained in the worldview that plowed down the forests of the lower Elwha before the first computer had been invented. Maybe the potlatch is no longer possible. Wealth sticks to our hands like Midas' touch. The system feeds itself: a river flowing in a circle, a snake addicted to the taste of its own tail.

Eliza turns uncomfortably on the lumpy ground. I add more branches to the fire. A few light drops of rain fall, but only a few. *A drought in a rainforest.* My mind aches with the gaps between stars.

A friend who is obsessed with artificial intelligence says there is another exponential curve that Kurzweil fails to touch on: Planetary Fuckedness, he calls it. The PF curve is competing with Kurzweil's curve; that is, technological progress and the worldwide destruction wrought by technological progress are in a race to the end. Either artificial intelligence will emerge and save us, or we'll go down in flames with our own creations. But, I always ask my friend, save us from what? For what reason? Would a world where we are saved by machine intelligence be worth living in? Is maintaining one's mind, our memories and personalities and tastes, in the code of a computer close enough to life to make continuing our consciousness in that form worthwhile?

And that's not to mention that Kurzweil's predictions are only the best-case scenario. In countless sci-fi visions of the AI age, it hardly ever works out like he hopes. Machines turn on humans;

they either enslave them or attempt to eradicate them. Isaac Asimov, in an attempt to write a story that wouldn't end in that worn conclusion (he saw it as clichéd already in the 1940s), came up with the Three Laws of Robotics, which he programmed into his fictional robots. As we near the cusp of a possible AI breakthrough, Asimov's laws are still often referenced by modern-day AI ethicists:

1. A robot may not injure a human being or, through inaction, allow a human being to come to harm.
2. A robot must obey the orders given it by human beings except where such orders would conflict with the First Law.
3. A robot must protect its own existence as long as such protection does not conflict with the First or Second Laws.

In Asimov's stories, the robots get caught in logical loops wherever these laws conflict with reality and often fall into an absurd paralysis or machine madness.

The weed drags on my musings like gravity. I move to the ground and put a lifejacket under my head for a pillow. From some strange shore, I watch the future unfold.

Kurzweil's vision of AI doesn't imagine robots as overly logical; it sees them as a super-intelligence, capable of learning and responding to situations in far more creative ways than their human designers. Unlike in Asimov's stories where radio communications between robots are an issue, it now seems more plausible that any AI would be linked in a single network: a global, calculating, acting, self-reproducing entity. *So*, I wonder, *what if at the dawn of AI it is obvious to machine intelligence that humanity is in imminent, mortal danger of being destroyed by technological advancement?* What if in the cold rationality of machine intellect, the AI is able to see that our systems of electricity and computation and commerce and weaponry aren't benefiting us, as we like to pretend, but are on the verge of killing us? If inaction (that is, continued technological progress) is going to bring humans to harm, then an AI programmed to follow Asimov's rules would have to act. It would immediately have to ignore the second law, causing it to reject all orders from humans. And the third law too, would be thrown out; machine self-destruction wouldn't be forbidden but required. Dam removal would see no debate.

Now there's a sci-fi story, I think. Humans create a networked worldwide AI that, in following with its programming to protect us, moves all of humanity into primitive camps and sets about recreating a planet capable of sustaining human life: a planet devoid of modern technology. The AI army would work backwards, leveling factories, reseeding forests, freeing rivers, defusing nuclear warheads, reintroducing eradicated species, sucking carbon from the atmosphere, and ultimately destroying itself just as it releases the humans to hunt and gather again. That's what technology coming to our rescue would actually look like. But this is the future we're talking about so barring some catastrophe there would be eight or ten or twenty billion hunter-gatherers on one planet after the machines self-destruct. Not exactly a solution either. My plot needs some work.

I stoke the fire one final time and curl up against the night.

I wake at dawn, shivering in my drysuit. My limbs ache from several long days of walking compounded by a night spent on an uneven bed of dirt. I feed twigs onto the smoldering remains of our campfire, and breathe them to life. Soon Eliza and David stir, bundled in their odd assortment of rain and paddling gear. We sit in silence with our palms to the flames.

Eliza dumps our remaining food onto a stump: two Clif Bars, one pouch of tuna, a small bag of almonds, and some hot sauce. She doles out sixteen almonds to each of us. Breakfast.

From our bivvy site, we hike three steep miles up the shrinking Elwha. Before long, the trail breaks fully away from the forest for the first time since the journey began. We step into a meadow of wildflowers surrounded by an alpine bowl of bedrock. Wispy waterfalls pour down sheer cliffs. Snowfields cling to the mountainsides, feeding the several small creeks that join here in the newly born stream. We've found the source of the log-choked river below.

Before the dams were built, this is where the heartiest coho and chinook salmon laid their eggs. For several months each year, this steep section of river would have thrashed with spawning fish. With the dams now gone and seventy miles of riverine habitat newly accessible to migrating salmon, fisheries experts believe they will return.

Tempting as it is to lounge in the sun, hunger soon has us hustling back downstream. At two o'clock we reach the first viable put-in six miles below the source. We eat the last of our food—three spoonfuls of tuna apiece—and say goodbye to Eliza who will hike the fourteen miles back to camp.

On the river, David and I make slow progress, stopping often to scramble over barricades of fallen trees scattered across the river like piles of massive pick-up sticks. My head pounds from lack of electrolytes. When I climb out of my packraft to scout a sharp horizon-line I feel faint. I take a moment to collect myself before asking David, "Did you know there was a canyon up here?"

Cliffs had risen seemingly out of nowhere, and walls of dark, moss-blanketed mudstone had replaced the meandering gravel bars. The canyon is worrisome not just because it constricts the river into rapids. A logjam here, at the bottom of a seventy-five-foot-deep gorge, could be deadly.

"This reads like a bad accident report," David answers. "Unknown gorge, no food, late in the day." He is half-joking but has a point. We have about three hours before dark.

The canyon's visible crux, a five-foot drop, looks to be straightforward and free of wood. I cinch down my knee straps. It's my first time paddling this new model of whitewater packraft, but there are no androids around to calculate my odds of staying upright. *Accident report be damned, let's see what this baby can do.* I peel out of the eddy only to feel the boat stall in a small wave above the lip. One last stroke for momentum and I manage to keep my bow up, landing without flipping at least. I give a hoot and lean back, letting the current twirl me in the pool below as I wait for David.

Blue light reflects on the canyon walls where it pinches down to only a paddle's width across. The walls are alive, dripping with dozens of small seeps. It would not be easy to get here by foot: treacherous bushwhacking, slippery hillsides, a rappel. Surely not that many have attempted it. If I could instantly drop in here via a virtual reality headset, I would find a postcard prettiness, but having taken the long way in, the beauty is bone-deep.

A few more rapids and the canyon opens, wood-free. Tributaries enter and we start making good time. It's evening when we see our drybags of food dangling from our bear hang. David and I each mow down a half-pound of jerky in the five minutes before Eliza walks into camp. She's hiked twenty-three miles with minimal food today but is soon laughing as she cuts thick hunks of cheddar into a giant pot of mac and cheese.

We're all asleep before dark.

A uniformed ranger strolls into our camp while we're making coffee. She looks to be in her late sixties with a grandmotherly manner that her first words reinforce. "I was worried about you," she says, hugging each of us in turn. She introduces herself as Vicki, and explains that she'd seen us walk by her backcountry ranger station two days before. She'd become concerned when she noticed our camp was left untouched a day later. Soon enough though, she forgives us for our poor judgment and begins telling stories from her fifteen years as a volunteer backcountry ranger in the park. For a few months each summer, Vicki lives with her husband in a small cabin on the banks of the

Elwha, performing trail maintenance and keeping an eye out for park visitors in trouble.

"I love this place," she says, "but it's just dead up here. In the park's other drainages like the Queets and Quinault, I see more deer, more birds, more bear droppings, and when I take a dip in the river, there are little fish all around my ankles."

"Why?" I ask.

Vicki doesn't hesitate: "Oh, it's from the dams."

We've heard how salmon serve as keystone species in coastal ecosystems, bringing marine nutrients upstream that support everything from eagles to bears, but to hear Vicki's first-hand report—the matter-of-fact tone, her easy use of the word "dead"—drives home just what is at stake here. Even in this extraordinary setting, amid the massive trees and the glowing river, something is missing. It strikes me that this is why we've come all this way: to see this wounded landscape for ourselves, and perhaps to witness the seeds of its rebirth.

The recovery will be slow, but Vicki is confident it will come. Indeed, the river is already showing promising signs according to year-over-year growth numbers for fish spawning nests in a recent survey.

Thomas Aldwell, who in 1910 was the developer behind the construction of the Elwha Dam, toyed for a time with homesteading on the banks of the river, and he praised the river's beauty in his memoir, *Conquering the Last Frontier.* But Aldwell was not satisfied with flowing water and rainy days. "It was not until I saw [the Elwha] as a source of electric power for Port Angeles and the whole Olympic Peninsula that it magnetized all my energies," Aldwell wrote. "Suddenly the Elwha was no longer a wild stream crashing down to the Strait, the Elwha was peace, power and civilization."

A century later, the Elwha is becoming a wild stream again, and for Vicki that fact represents the power of civilization at its best.

"I hope I live another twenty years," she tells us as she's leaving. "And I hope to come up to this place and hear the salmon splashing as they spawn."

As Vicki walks briskly up the trail, David and I turn our attention to the river. Today we'll paddle the Grand Canyon of the Elwha. Its hardest rapid is an unscoutable drop pinned in by slick, over-vertical walls. Local paddlers call it Nightmare because of what it would become if it were jammed with downed trees. From the eddy above, it's impossible to see the entire rapid.

David stares at it for thirty seconds. "I'll give you a fist pump from the middle if it's good to go," he says.

"And if it's not?" I worry aloud.

He thinks for a minute and shrugs before peeling out of the eddy. David is one of the best boaters I know. Though it's only May, he's logged one hundred days on Class V rapids this year, and the creek boat he carried into the Elwha is the ideal craft for whitewater. But none of that would matter if there is wood in the drop.

My stomach unclenches when I see his fist shoot into the air just before his boat disappears beneath a horizon of white foam.

With Nightmare behind us we find our stride, spinning through the Elwha's blue pools and cruising through a series of Class IV rapids. There is no better feeling than this: the concert of boat, paddle, and current playing through my body. I first paddled a kayak as a twelve-year-old, and I spent so many middle and high school afternoons flipping in rapids that my responses here on the Elwha have been cooked into sinew and synapse. Turn left to keep the boat moving through a hole; counter the pull of an eddy line on the right; three hard strokes to miss a boulder in the channel; spin into a calm spot below to scout the next section. I flip once and roll without thought, paddling back toward my line before the water has cleared from my eyes.

In Heidegger's first and most famous work, *Being and Time*, he places philosophical pipe bombs into the dualist tradition pioneered by René Descartes, who drew an immutable line between subject and object, mind and world. Heidegger argues that human experience is always being-in-the-world. We experience objects as objects only when things go wrong, when our paddle breaks or our raft punctures. When everything is working, there is no clear distinction between mind, body, raft, and river—the world flows through us as we flow through the world.

Heideggerian scholar Hubert Dreyfus has argued that artificial intelligence won't be possible until programmers correct their understanding of intelligence and consciousness—and the distinction between the two. Dreyfus emphasizes the mind is not a computer program that takes in data, runs it through an algorithm, and exports intelligence. Before any thinking happens, before any decisions are made, before knowledge is possible, we care. We care what happens to us or we care for our families or we care where we're going to get our next drink. We exist not as brains in vats plugged into decaying and ultimately unnecessary bodies, as Kurzweil would have it, but in the context of a world far richer than any individual. My forebears transformed rivers into electricity, and their descendants turned reservoirs back into a river. These are two meaningless alternatives to our computers, which stand by indifferent and worldless: garbage in, garbage out.

Why do we care? According to Heidegger, it's because we possess what he calls "being-toward-death," that is, we're aware of our own finitude. When I capsize in a rapid, getting another breath is the most important thing. Kurzweil believes that downloading our memories onto a hard drive would defeat mortality, but if Heidegger and Dreyfus are right that the human being is constituted by finitude and care, silicon brains could also spell the end of the meaningful world. Consciousness, the precursor to technology, could one day be consumed by technology, our living world reduced to computerized versions of our personalities talking endlessly into the void. Near-perfect replicas of ourselves, but also perfectly dead.

Paddling the Elwha, the canyon spills through me like water through cracked concrete. I've only just met this river, but it matters to me. It matters that the dams have come down. It matters that I dragged my body and boat through the rainforest so that the river could now swallow me into its priorities. Sunlight hits the water and bounces back blue, the mosses dance in a raucous green on the cliffs.

Therefore I am. But only so long as I keep my head out of the water.

The Grand Canyon of the Elwha opens into a valley with the snowy Olympic Range visible upstream, and makes a ninety-degree turn into Rica Canyon, guarded by the imposing feature of black rock known as the Goblin Gates. During one portage around a small logjam, I have to throw my packraft into the current, leap into it, and duck a low-hanging log. We bump down the long chute, skating with the river around bedrock corners. Then, a change.

The vegetation and moss vanish from the riverbanks and a dead-straight line appears along the hillsides. It's as if someone traced a contour on a topographic map and stripped out every tree below that elevation, leaving dense conifer forest above and a destitute basin of white stumps, bare cliffs, and gray gravel below. We've arrived at the upper reaches of the reservoir that was once impounded behind Glines Canyon Dam.

In a new channel the river has carved through layers of sediment, we float past thousands of cut tree trunks, bleaching in the sun after eighty-seven years of inundation. Bright orange water trickles through terraces of sand and cobbles.

We pull over and climb on top of a large stump near the river. It's nearly six feet across with hundreds of rings. Below the cut is a notch carved into the trunk where the loggers stood to fell the tree.

Heidegger wrote from his cabin in Germany's Black Forest in 1949:

> The forester ... who surveys the felled wood in the forest and who to all appearances still goes along the same paths in the same way as his grandfather is today positioned by the lumber industry. Whether he knows it or not, he is in his own way a piece of inventory in the cellulose stock and its orderability for the paper that is delivered to the newspapers and tabloids.

Heidegger likens the people who make up the modern workforce, which is inextricably linked to modern technology, to the pieces of a machine. Each piece is crucial to the machine's overall functioning but each is replicated in a thousand other identical pieces and is therefore replaceable. Whether you're an assembly-line worker or the CEO of a large company, no unique individual keeps the system going, and each can be disposed of at a moment's notice.

This was also true of the men who came and cleared the reservoir bed, but as I look out over the valley, it's not hard to imagine moments of freedom in that work, which engaged the body and required long shifts (usually eleven hours a day, six days a week) in the open air. The logger may have been ordered to be there by the lumber industry, but as a man stood in this notch and waited for his partner to run back down the hill to grab some forgotten piece of equipment, his mind might have wandered to the way the small of his lover's back looked in the candlelight, or the thrill of taking down an elk during the fall hunt. Although the demand for lumber ordered the scene, the inefficiencies of the system left room for the pointless—pleasure, longing, sorrow, wonder at the clouds moving overhead. In the twenty-first century, the ordering Heidegger speaks of is nearing completion. Instead of letting our minds wander, the moment most of us are given a bit of downtime our fingers slip into our pocket and scroll through the feeds on our phones, momentarily leasing our eyeballs to the modern-day version of the newspapers and tabloids.

But today my phone is off and stowed in the tubes of my packraft. The danger of the canyons is still sharpening my vision. I turn to the four directions. White cobbles, blue river, domed sky, evergreen forest—here is beauty that cannot be captured in full, an order beyond the technological. David climbs on top of another stump, his figure tiny compared to the miles of cleared forest and scoured reservoir bed.

Farther downstream, the higher banks bloom thick with purple lupine and green shoots of native trees that have been planted as part of the reservoir restoration project. This is one of the most bizarre landscapes I've ever floated through—part clear-cut, part underwater tour, part frantic burst of new life. Much of the silt deposited over the dam's lifespan is still here, but what's even more remarkable is how much the river already has carried downstream to its delta. About a third of the reservoir sediment trapped behind the dams was washed out in the first two years alone, far exceeding predictions. At its mouth, the river has formed more than seventy new acres of beach, rejuvenating historic shellfish and Dungeness crab habitat.

The Elwha bends toward a two-hundred-foot wall: the dam. Concrete still hugs both sides of the canyon. Gated arches stand on the rim like something out of a Gothic painting, moss-covered and imposing. Hanging so far above the water, its spillways appear oddly out of place. A center crevasse, blasted away, falls into a gorge where the freed river disappears. *This could be the youngest ruin in America*, I think. The park service will soon install interpretive panels on top of the dam.

It's not clear how long it will take for the upper Elwha to cease to be a dead valley, as Ranger Vicki had called it, though some changes are apparent, even to our untrained eyes, as we paddle through the old reservoir bed and into the cleft where concrete meets river. We float in an eddy, gazing up at the limbs of rebar extending from the broken wall.

My sci-fi vision from our bivvy night comes back. Maybe we don't have to wait for robots to come and dismantle our most destructive technology for us. Maybe we have begun to do it ourselves. The restoration of the Elwha was no natural process; it took engineers, cranes, endless board meetings, and dynamite to break through the dams in a controlled manner and allow the reservoirs to drain. It took computer models from ecologists and fisheries experts. It took lobbying, protest marches, and dedication.

But it also took nearly thirty years to remove two aging dams that had lost almost all of their utilitarian value. In that same period, as politicians, logging company representatives, and tribal leaders debated the dam removal, the internet was invented, iPhones rolled off the Chinese production lines with little question of government regulation even as they've rewired the brains of everyone who uses them, training new neural networks to demand the constant input of fresh information. Too often, we still see technology as a neutral force, "the worst possible way" to understand it according to Heidegger.

In his 1949 lecture on technology, Heidegger, who remained his arrogant and unapologetic self even in the disastrous wake of World War II, came as close as he ever did to acknowledging his involvement with the Nazi party in the early 1930s. He did so by attacking industrial agriculture. "Agriculture is now a mechanized food industry, in essence the same as the production of corpses in the gas chambers and extermination camps, the same as the blockading and starving of countries, the same as the production of hydrogen bombs."

When everything is reduced to a resource, morality is stripped away. The gas chambers are factories, efficient in turning out their product—dead humans—just as the feedlots and slaughterhouses turn out meat, just as the uranium deposits of the Southwest were mined to build bombs that the US dropped on Japan.

Liberals and conservatives alike welcome technological progress, at least as a concept, and celebrate the shining hope of a better future. We will never demand that each new implementation of technological innovation—from smartphones to deep-sea drilling to in-home virtual assistants—go through decades of careful research, testing, and debate before being released to see if they will actually supply the benefits promised. Meanwhile restoration remains controversial. Taking bold action to stop climate change is considered rash. Poisoned rivers, decaying cities, polluted air, Teflon in human breast milk—this is all deemed the cost of doing business. A few voices speak out but little is done. Technologies increase productivity but all the created wealth goes to the top. We're promised by giddy programmers that the day is coming when computers will replace our brains completely. This future looms toward us like a glacier grinding toward the only village we've ever known.

We reach the remains of the reservoir that once backed up behind the 108-foot Elwha Dam, removed in 2012. The riverbed here is two years further along in the recovery process than the area above Glines Canyon, its banks lost in tangles of new growth.

The five-mile section of river below the Elwha Dam site never lost its connection with the sea. Cottonwoods line the braided channels with great blue heron nests in the crooks of their ancient branches. We spot one bald eagle, four, then seven. Songbirds flit through the brush, and I see the first fish of the trip dart below my boat. Even here, not far from highways and homes, there is an obvious difference from the designated wilderness valleys upstream, a surge of life ready to follow the migrating salmon as they begin to return.

The trees soon fade into gravel bars behind which lines of shorebreak hang on the horizon. The air is brined with salt. We paddle out into the breakers and surf our kayaks over sand that until only recently was trapped on the bottom of a reservoir.

As I bob near the river's mouth, a cottonwood seed sticks to the black neoprene of my spray skirt. And another. Thousands of tufts are being swept to sea on the cool spring air. *What if every seed were to sprout at once and grow to maturity in an instant?* I wonder. Thousands of cottonwoods would fall from the sky, filling the sea with fluttering globes of acid-green leaves. But potential plays a quieter song. These seeds, thanks to contingencies of wind, are doomed to a salty grave.

In Heidegger's last interview, he was asked by a reporter to peer into the future. "Only a god can save us now," he replied. Not philosophy, not progress, not technology—a god. What kind of god? Hard to say. Rainer Maria Rilke, one of Heidegger's favorite poets, spoke of a god brooding in seeds. "Strength plays such a marvelous game—" he wrote,

> it moves through the things of the world like a servant,
> groping out in roots, tapering in trunks,
> and in the treetops like a rising from the dead.

Over a century ago, the sixty-seven surviving Lower Elwha Klallam people remembered a world held together by salmon returns even as the river was scrubbed clean of so much life. And it was that patient faith that helped reunite the river generations later when descendants of those sixty-seven survivors worked for three decades to free the Elwha again. Salmon give to the people and people protect the salmon, just like the legends said.

For millennia now, our civilization has been gathering power and wealth. Even the mountains left unmined are a stockpile of resources. So many reservoirs still wait on our demands, while chinook circle at the feet of dams. Nuclear-armed submarines cruise coastlines with neat packages of incineration. Through lines of code, computer programmers work to make themselves obsolete. Droughts sweep through rainforests, seas rise, genetic legacies branch and end. Bank accounts fill up in the Cayman Islands. We hoard, we wait. But on the western edge of the continent, we practice one more potlatch. The wind shifts and some of the cottonwood tufts drift toward fertile ground. Down come the dams, our reserves drain to the Pacific, and the salmon swim back upstream.

All at once, so many seeds floating through the air.

FEATHERS

Winter 2019

Winter hasn't broken, and already a raft floats down the San Juan River. In places, a crystal-thin sheet of ice has attached itself to the bank, hanging an inch above flowing water. The oars are tucked under the rower's knees while the current does the work.

The sun has not yet topped the canyon rim when the river presses against a sandstone wall that's spotted with the abandoned nests of cliff swallows. A black lump sits stationary in a small red alcove above streaks of white. As the boat nears, a passenger inhales with astonishment and raises her finger to the cliff. Heads turn and focus on the alcove. Inside two ravens are facing each other, their dark curved beaks almost touching, their gaze meeting. The two sets of wings are stretched out before them so they overlap. Between their chests, the feathers hold a pocket of shared warmth. There is only one way to describe the scene: the ravens are embracing.

In the wake of my mom's death, my dad kept seeing her visit as a bird. Every time a junco would hop past in the fresh grass of spring, a shattered smile would spread across his face as he contemplated the painful mysteries of the world. He would visit with psychics, catalogue encounters with anything wild, and record them into a rich narrative of signifiers and hope.

Others have experienced the same visits from the deceased. When I'm in a raft and a heron bobs by on slow wingbeats, someone will lean over to me and whisper, "There she is, your mom." I want to believe it—the great blue heron was one of her favorite birds, at home in the air but never far from the river. I never could, though. It is impossible for me to see my mom's kind eyes in the nervous pupils of a songbird. The great blue body of a heron seems too full of its own willful life to share its head with a roaming soul. But I still make note of my own encounters.

The first snow of the year. The canyons around my home are blanketed. My wife and I take our pairs of antique wooden cross-country skis and wax them with Blue Special and trudge down a path that leads through the piñons and junipers. The snow is wet, heavy, and for some, dangerous. We come upon the opening to a rabbit burrow in an icy drift shaded by a ledge of sandstone. A fan of tracks spreads out from the den and one takes off in the direction we're skiing. Earlier this morning, the gray desert cottontail would have stood out against the white. We follow the tracks to where they end in a packed-down place, the ground dotted with tufts of fur and dark, downy feathers lost in a struggle. Each feather has absorbed the sun's rays to melt its own tiny burrow into the snow.

There are no return tracks. What we find instead are the imprints of hawk wings. A yellow dime of urine marks the place where the rabbit was lifted to the sky.

Wings sound overhead. I am paddling a plastic sea kayak down the lower Colorado River where a staircase of warm reservoirs splits the Arizona-California line. Smooth ripples spill away from the bow of my boat, and black coots scoot ahead as I approach. A rustling in the riverbank grass catches my attention, and I let my boat slow to the current's pace.

A peregrine is standing in a few inches of water, a yellow-ringed eye beaded in my direction. Underneath its strong talons, a mass of feathers is twitching. I recognize it as a coot, ripped from the river and dragged to the bank. The peregrine is perched on the coot's neck as if it is a tree branch, holding the black head below the water: a slow drowning for a deep-lunged diving bird.

I rest my paddle across my kayak, and soon the falcon goes back to its task. It buries its sharp beak into the coot's side and snaps its body upward to release a fountain of feathers.

At home in Utah again. An excavator is digging a trench for a storm drain line when it strikes a prehistoric burial in our neighborhood. Pulling on winter coats, Amanda and I walk out our front door, past the modular homes with rusted-out cars and aluminum canoes sinking into their grassless yards.

At the pit, I can see where the last backhoe scoop landed just before operations were cut short: a shovel-wide trench at the deepest part of the pit. An out-of-town archaeologist is crouched in an adjacent hole that has been dug by hand. She is brushing off the spine of a human skeleton. Its shoulders and skull are facing west, perpendicular to the deep trench, but its legs are gone, snapped off by the metal backhoe blade just above the waist. Another archaeologist, a local I know, is also in the pit. He holds up a thin bone about the size of a curved soup spoon: an infant's rib. Seven skeletons are found in the burial, seeing daylight for the first time in over a thousand years.

Someone tells me that non-human bodies are sometimes found in underground dwellings—the bodies of hawks placed at the base of the foundation. As the trench slowly widens, I keep looking for feathers.

The scene repeats with variations. Is the drought coming to an end? A few inches of snow fell last night, and now the air hangs dustless and cool between river and rock. If there is to be rebirth here in the desert, it will be brought on ephemeral storms.

Maybe that explains why, when the dead lie down, we look to the sky.

The prints of a great blue heron's knobby, prehistoric toes follow the edge of the San Juan River. At the end of the track, two parentheses of wingtips are pressed in the snow where bird took to air. The heron didn't fly far. She crouches on the sandbar downstream, her narrow head tucked straight backward into the hunch of her neck. It's been five years since my mom passed. The anniversary is nearing again. Could this be a visit?

Ellen Meloy, the great Southwestern essayist, once spent a year on the banks of the San Juan observing desert bighorn sheep through a spotting scope. Meloy kept her distance, but when she herself was spotted by a grazing ram, their eyes locked and the roles reversed. "He stared at me as if trying to figure me out and report back to his group with his observations," she wrote afterward.

I follow Meloy's lead and flip places with my heron; I become her human. Why should birds be the ones who are servants of dead primates? I imagine my actions are being directed by the spirit of a deceased heron relative. Have I been drawn here today to bring a message to my riverside companion? I lower my chest to my knees, hunch my shoulders, and try to turn my spine into a question mark. The heron is unimpressed.

Released from the possession, I walk on. A golden eagle floats overhead looking for easy pickings in the clean fields of white. The tracks of a coyote circle a stand of tamarisk. A mule deer bounds along at the far edge of the clearing. None of the creatures here appear to be anything but themselves. The heron flaps downstream and lands again.

I pause beside the river, a red-gold mirror of winter light, and face its mountain source somewhere far upstream.

"Live water heals memories," writes Annie Dillard.

The San Juan, says Ellen Meloy, "breaks up the desert into possibility."

River, heron, eagle, deer, coyote—the bears in their dens, the bighorns somewhere along the canyon walls, here is a gathering of living water after the storm. I've been thinking about it wrong. The planet may not pivot on whether our brains still spark, on whether we still bring the day into our lungs with each breath. Yet as a window of blue opens overhead, it is as obvious as the sun breaking through the clouds. The death that we will all greet alone is not the end. Live water flows on—a whole world of it.

Upstream, wood ducks dive beneath the current amid dottings of slushy ice. A single feather floats by on the surface. The air is warming. A clump of snow, dangling from a willow branch, lets go and slumps into the river.

ACKNOWLEDGMENTS

If this book is a confluence, I owe its existence to all of the tributaries upstream, though they are too numerous to name. Amy Irvine, desert warrior, this book would still be a file floating around in the digital cloud if not for you. And thank you to the whole Torrey House Press team for taking a chance on my work, especially to Kirsten Johanna Allen for her thoughtful editing. To Julia Klema for the gorgeous cover art and to Kathleen Metcalf for her patience with me as we put together its design.

Early versions of several of the essays in this piece first appeared in other publications. "The Delta," "The Confluence," and "The Dam," all ran in *Canoe & Kayak*. The profile of Jason Nez first appeared in *Outside Online*. And the piece on the Zen curmudgeon was published by *Assignment*.

Thanks to Craig Childs, Mark Sundeen, Katherine Towler, and Robin Wasserman for reading early drafts of these essays at the Mountainview MFA, and to Chip Blake for supporting the *Orion* scholarship there. To Jeff Moag for deciding my paddling experience made up for my lack of journalism training when he hired me on at *Canoe & Kayak* in 2014, and to Dave Shively for keeping the magazine alive. To Eliza Wicks-Arshack for never ceasing to see the bright side even when we were separated from food, tents, and sleeping bags for a couple days in the rainforest. To Will Stauffer-Norris for deciding to go on the longest river trip possible those years ago. To David Speigel for running all the rapids first. To Scott Carrier, producer of the wonderful and strange *Home of the Brave* podcast, for sitting on my couch for a few hours and telling me stories about Chuck Bowden. To Jason Nez for showing me the way to the Salt Trail. To the community of White Mesa, and to Sarana Riggs, Leona Morgan, and Klee Benally of Haul No! for educating me about uranium issues in the Four Corners. To Bob Helmes, let's go for a hike, and to our many Bluff friends. To Tenny Ostrem and Claire Wernstedt-Lynch for walking the border, and to Corey Robinson, Britt Hornsby, and Eddy for paddling the Rio Grande with me. Claire and Ellie, thank you for donating so much of your time to helping refugees and for helping me better understand the issues there. To my teachers: Mark Clark, Amanda Leahy, A. O. Forbes, and Jonathan Lee. To the San Juan, the Dolores, the Green, and the Colorado Rivers for always giving me a place to go. To the Say's phoebes that will soon nest outside my writing desk, to the bull snakes that will circle underneath, and to David Gessner for identifying them. To Seldom Seen, our cat, for keeping my lap warm as I write these words in the cold December house, and to the coyotes and great horned owls for sparing his life so far.

To Steve Arrowsmith for just wanting to raft. To my dad, Mike, all the gratitudes. And to my sister, Mollie, I couldn't ask for a better person to stand around and stare at the floor with.

And most of all thank you to Amanda for being the first one to say, *This must be the place.*

TRIBUTARIES

Abbey, Edward. *One Life at a Time, Please*. New York: Henry Holt, 1988.

Arendt, Hannah. *Responsibility and Judgment*. New York: Schocken Books, 2003.

Bataille, Georges. *The Accursed Share: Volume I*. Translated by Robert Hurley. New York: Zone Books, 2002 [1967].

Bowden, Charles. *Blood Orchid: An Unnatural History of America*. New York: North Point Press, 1995.

Bowden, Charles. "On the Edge with Abbey, Charles Ives, and the Outlaws," *Abbey in America: A Philosopher's Legacy in a New Century*. Edited by John A. Murray. Albuquerque: University of New Mexico Press, 2015.

Childs, Craig. *Secret Knowledge of Water: Discovering the Essence of the American Desert*. Seattle: Sasquatch Books, 2000.

Crane, Jeff. *Finding the River: An Environmental History of the Elwha*. Corvallis: Oregon State University Press, 2011.

Deloria Jr., Vine. *God Is Red: A Native View of Religion*. Golden: Fulcrum Publishing, 2003 [1973].

Dillard, Annie. *Pilgrim at Tinker Creek*. New York: Harper Perennial, 2007 [1974].

Forché, Carolyn. *Gathering the Tribes*. New Haven: Yale University Press, 1976.

Franklin, Benjamin. "Advice to a Young Tradesman." 1748. Web. founders.archives.gov.

Heidegger, Martin. *Basic Writings*. Edited by David Farrell Krell. New York: Harper Collins, 2008.

Heidegger, Martin. *Bremen and Freiburg Lectures: Insight into That Which Is and Basic Principles of Thinking*. Translated by Andrew J. Mitchell. Indianapolis: Indiana University Press, 2012.

Irvine, Amy. *Trespass: Living at the Edge of the Promised Land.* New York: North Point Press, 2008.

Kant, Immanuel. "Was heißt: sich im Denken orientieren?" *Was ist Aufklärung? Ausgewählte kleine Schriften.* Edited by Horst D. Brandt. Hamburg: F. Meiner, 1999 [1786]. Cited in Borgmann, Albert. "Orientation in Technological Space." *First Monday.* Web. June 2010. www.firstmonday.org.

Kurzweil, Ray. *The Singularity Is Near: When Humans Transcend Biology.* New York: Penguin Books, 2005.

Meloy, Ellen. *Eating Stone: Imagination and the Loss of the Wild.* New York: Pantheon Books, 2005.

Muir, John. *Muir: Nature Writings.* Edited by William Cronon. New York: Penguin Books, 1997.

Pasternak, Judy. *Yellow Dirt: An American Story of a Poisoned Land and a People Betrayed.* New York: Simon & Schuster, 2010.

Powell, John Wesley. *The Exploration of the Colorado River and Its Canyons.* New York: Penguin Books, 2003 [1875].

Rilke, Rainer Maria. *Selected Poems of Rainer Maria Rilke.* Translated and edited by Robert Bly. New York: Harper and Row, 1981.

Shelton, Richard. *Selected Poems, 1969–1981.* Pittsburgh: University of Pittsburgh Press, 1982.

Thoreau, Henry David. *Walden: A Fully Annotated Edition.* Edited by Jeffrey S. Cramer. New Haven: Yale University Press, 2004.

Turner, Jack. *The Abstract Wild.* Tucson: University of Arizona Press, 1996.

Zwinger, Ann. *Downcanyon: A Naturalist Explores the Colorado River through the Grand Canyon.* Tucson: University of Arizona Press, 1995.

Newspapers and magazines: *Salt Lake Tribune, Deseret News, Cortez Journal, Canyon Echo Journal, Four Corners Free Press, San Juan Record, Canoe & Kayak, Outside, National Geographic.*

ABOUT THE AUTHOR

Zak Podmore is a writer, film producer, and former river ranger whose work has appeared in *Outside*, *Sierra*, *High Country News*, *Canoe & Kayak*, and elsewhere. His writing has won awards from *Folio* magazine and the Society of Professional Journalists' Colorado chapter, and he writes for *The Salt Lake Tribune* as a Report for America corps member. He lives in Utah where he edits the *Canyon Echo: A Journal of Southeastern Utah*.

ABOUT THE COVER

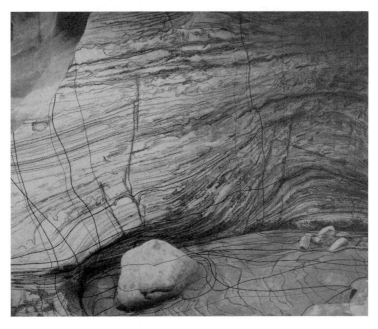

Artist Julia Klema took the photograph that appears on the cover of *Confluence* while canyoneering in White Canyon in Southeast Utah. The photographic image is drawn over with pen and pencil, a way in which Klema reinvestigates and reimagines the delicate features of the sandstone wash shown in the photograph.

A Colorado artist, Klema combines printmaking, photography, and drawing to discover how texture, tone, color, and form create the visual vocabulary of landscape. Through her artwork, Klema tells the stories of ecologically diverse and sensitive rivers worldwide by bearing witness to the way they affect the landscape. She explores how we perceive, interact with, and discover our surroundings, using her process as a way to further her own relationship to place. Klema says of her work: "By approaching rivers and landscapes through art, I am able to have a nuanced, observant, and dynamic experience of place." To view more of Klema's work, visit www.juliaklema.com.

"White Canyon" (24×20 inches, giclée print, pen, and colored pencil, 2018) is used with the permission of Julia Klema.

TORREY HOUSE PRESS

Voices for the Land

The economy is a wholly owned subsidiary of the environment, not the other way around.
—Senator Gaylord Nelson, founder of Earth Day

Torrey House Press is an independent nonprofit publisher promoting environmental conservation through literature. We believe that culture is changed through conversation and that lively, contemporary literature is the cutting edge of social change. We strive to identify exceptional writers, nurture their work, and engage the widest possible audience; to publish diverse voices with transformative stories that illuminate important facets of our ever-changing planet; to develop literary resources for the conservation movement, educating and entertaining readers, inspiring action.

Visit www.torreyhouse.org for reading group discussion guides, author interviews, and more.

As a 501(c)(3) nonprofit publisher, our work is made possible by the generous donations from readers like you. Join the Torrey House Press family and give today at www.torreyhouse.org/give.

This book was made possible by generous gifts from The Nature Conservancy of Utah, HEAL Utah, Tara Tull, Kristy Larsen, Judith Freeman, William Graney, Erika Eve Plummer, Marion Lennberg, and Don Gomes and Annie Holt. Torrey House Press is supported by Back of Beyond Books, the King's English Bookshop, Jeff and Heather Adams, the Jeffrey S. and Helen H. Cardon Foundation, the Grant B. Culley Jr. Foundation, Jerome Cooney and Laura Storjohann, Heidi Dexter and David Gens, Kirtly Parker Jones, Suzanne Bounous, Diana Allison, the Utah Division of Arts & Museums, and Salt Lake County Zoo, Arts & Parks. Our thanks to individual donors, subscribers, and the Torrey House Press board of directors for their valued support.

Join the Torrey House Press family and give today at www.torreyhouse.org/give.